I0481290

Investing in Cryptocurrency

The Ultimate Guide About Blockchain, Mining, Trading, ICO, Ethereum Platform, Exchanges, Top Cryptocurrencies for Investing, and Perfect Strategies to Make Money

© Copyright 2018 by _____ - All rights reserved.

The following eBook is reproduced below with the goal of providing information that is as accurate and reliable as possible. Regardless, purchasing this eBook can be seen as consent to the fact that both the publisher and the author of this book are in no way experts on the topics discussed within and that any recommendations or suggestions that are made herein are for entertainment purposes only. Professionals should be consulted as needed prior to undertaking any of the action endorsed herein.

This declaration is deemed fair and valid by both the American Bar Association and the Committee of Publishers Association and is legally binding throughout the United States.

Furthermore, the transmission, duplication or reproduction of any of the following work including specific information will be considered an illegal act irrespective of if it is done electronically or in print. This extends to creating a secondary or tertiary copy of the work or a recorded copy and is only allowed with express written consent from the Publisher. All additional rights reserved.

The information in the following pages is broadly considered to be a truthful and accurate account of facts and as such any inattention, use or misuse of the information in question by the reader will render any resulting actions solely under their purview. There are no scenarios in which the publisher or the original author of this work can be in any fashion deemed liable for any hardship or damages that may befall them after undertaking information described herein.

Additionally, the information in the following pages is intended only for informational purposes and should thus be thought of as universal. As befitting its nature, it is presented without assurance regarding its prolonged validity or interim quality. Trademarks that are mentioned are done without written consent and can in no way be considered an endorsement from the trademark holder.

Table of Contents

Introduction

Congratulations on downloading this book and thank you for doing so.

The following chapters will discuss everything that you need to know to get started with investing in cryptocurrencies. Cryptocurrencies are relatively new to the market, and there are still so many people who have never even heard about them, much less used these currencies to start with. This means that there is a lot of potentials out there for investors who are ready to jump into the market and see some great results. This guidebook will provide you with all the information you need to be successful with investing in cryptocurrency.

In the first section of this book, we will talk about some of the basics of cryptocurrency. We will talk about some of the big players in the game, how to get started with your own exchange site, what the blockchain is, and everything else that you need to know to get started with these currencies.

Then we will move on to the second section, which will look more in depth at the big players in the cryptocurrency market. While the first section spent time talking in general, this section will talk about the names like Bitcoin, Ethereum, and more. In addition, we will take a look at how cryptocurrencies are doing, and if it is likely, they will stay around in the future.

And finally, the third section has everything that you need to know to get started with investing in these cryptocurrencies. We will not only discuss some of the different cryptocurrencies that are great for investing in, but we will also talk about some of the strategies that you can follow, how to tell when a currency is a good one to use, and how to pick out a safe and secure wallet.

There are so many different parts that come with investing in cryptocurrency. Understanding all of them can make a world of difference in how well your investing goes. When you are ready to learn everything that you need about investing in cryptocurrency, and you are ready to start making money in this market, take some time to read through this guidebook before getting started.

There are plenty of books on this subject on the market, thanks again for choosing this one! Every effort was made to ensure it is full of as much useful information as possible, please enjoy!

Part 1: What, How, and Why

Chapter 1: What is Cryptocurrency?

A cryptocurrency is a digital or virtual currency, one that often works similar to fiat money as a medium of exchange. While fiat currencies rely on a government agency to help keep them running, these cryptocurrencies will rely on cryptography to keep them secure, help to verify transactions, and to basically keep them running. In addition, this same cryptography will be used to help create some new units of a particular cryptocurrency.

One thing that is nice about these currencies is that you can use them similar to how you use fiat money for all your online transactions. As of right now, you are not able to use these currencies offline, meaning that it is not possible to print off paper versions of these currencies and then take the shopping with you. But, for those who like to shop online, those who want to invest, or those who need to send money to others no matter where they live throughout the world, these cryptocurrencies can help make it all happen.

Cryptocurrencies vs. Fiat Money

To help you learn more about cryptocurrencies and how they work, it helps to see the differences between these cryptocurrencies and the fiat money you are used to using. When we talk about fiat money, we are talking about the traditional money used in your country of origin. This is the money that you can go to the bank and get, the money that you can use to pay your bills or go and use at the grocery store.

This currency is considered valuable because the government is there to back it up. If the government, or another big agency in your country, took away their backing, the currency would become worthless. If something does go wrong in concerns to the currency, such as your bank going under, the government will be there to provide you with your funds, rather than you losing all your money.

Fiat currency is the currency that most people rely on. They like it when someone else can control the money and that someone is there to guarantee that the money will be worth something each day. However, some people wish the government would stay out of their transactions. They may feel that the government is not able to do a good job with controlling the money, or that the government has no business sticking their nose into their money. Many don't trust the government after all the issues that occurred with the economic downturn of 2008. These people would rather be in charge of their own money rather than letting the government take over it.

This is where cryptocurrency can come into the game. On the surface, cryptocurrencies work in similar manners as fiat currency in that you can use the online currency to make purchases. You can also send money to people in other countries and accept the currency as payment for your own goods or services. One noticeable difference though is that this is a currency that will only work online. You will never be able to print off this currency to use at a regular store, and there are a limited amount of online retailers who will accept cryptocurrencies at tis time.

The biggest difference in fiat currency and cryptocurrencies is that with cryptocurrencies, there are no central agencies that run the currency. You will not find any bank or government who runs the currency. Instead, they rely on mathematical equations and the blockchain technology to help it run. For many users, this is a benefit that helps them to complete the transactions that they want securely.

These mathematical equations are pretty challenging, which are meant to ensure the market keeps going without needing someone to come in and make changes. This can be a nice change to those who would like to keep their privacy when making purchases or doing other things online.

Are These Currencies Safe to Use?

Yes, it is completely safe to use these cryptocurrencies, as long as you take the proper precautions to make sure that no one can get ahold of your personal information. You must remember that there isn't a central authority in control of the currency so you won't have anyone to help you out if something goes wrong with the network or if a hacker gets into your account.

With that said, there are some safeguards to prevent hackers getting onto the network or from someone messing with the transactions that occur. Whether they are working on the blockchain or on the scrypt protocol, these cryptocurrencies are designed for all the computers on the system to agree before any changes can be made. Since the computers on the network are found all around the world, this is pretty near impossible.

You can further keep your currencies safe in other ways as well. You can choose a good wallet to secure the coins, backup your coins in case of a computer malfunction, and even monitor the market to make sure that no big downturns are about to happen with your chosen currency.

Are All Cryptocurrencies the Same?

No, all the cryptocurrencies are not the same. There are a few that are similar and can be used the same way. But with more than 1000 cryptocurrencies in the market, there wouldn't be enough room in the market for them to all work in the market.

There are a bunch of different uses for the various cryptocurrencies, which helps to make the market so interesting and fun to learn about. Some examples of how these cryptocurrencies can be used include:

Bitcoin: Bitcoin is a peer-to-peer payment system. You can only use the coins online, but for those who spend a lot of time shopping online, you may not notice a big difference between using Bitcoin and using your credit card. This system works with the blockchain and can help you to send and receive money instantly from anywhere in the word with limited transaction fees.

Ethereum: Ethereum is a platform that concentrates on expanding the blockchain technology. This platform offers an open sourced version of blockchain that anyone can use. People will use the ether, or the coin available on this network, to pay for fees and other thins while developing their blockchain app.

Ripple: Ripple is a network that helps people to send money to others, no matter where they are located in the world. You are actually able to use this currency with or without the coins, which makes it really easy for a lot of people to work with. Ripple can take any currency and move it throughout the world almost instantly. While it can help individuals with transactions, it is best known for helping move money for larger enterprises.

Litecoin: Litecoin is another peer-to-peer payment system like Bitcoin, but it has some different features that make it easier to use. It can get transactions done in two and a half minutes, rather than the ten minutes that it takes Bitcoin, and it contains more coins than Bitcoin to keep the network running. It is also an example of a scrypt cryptocurrency.

Dogecoin: Dogecoin is another option that works a bit differently than the others. This currency is used to tip people on social media or on their websites. When you like some of the content, you will send some of these coins over to the other person. These coins are not worth a whole lot right now, which is why they are known more as a tipping option rather than a payment option.

These are a few of the examples of how cryptocurrencies can be different. There are so many niches that these currencies can cover that there is still plenty of room for more to come into the market.

Who Accepts These Currencies?

Cryptocurrencies are relatively new. Because of this, the list of retailers that accept these coins as a form of payment is not as big as some users may like. With that being said, there are still a number of places that will take these coins, and some of them are major retailers.

Bitcoin is one of the most widely accepted cryptocurrencies out there. The list of companies that currency accept Bitcoin and it will grow into the future. These retailers include both in store and online stores. All the companies that accept Bitcoin and the other cryptocurrencies will include a payment button on their website (and they usually advertise this fact), so it is easy for you to see it right away.

In some cases, you may find that some local companies accept Bitcoin in their stores. Using your Bitcoin, even though you can't print off paper versions of the coin, is easy. You just need to add an app to your smartphone that will provide you with a barcode. Inside this barcode, you will have information on your private key. The company simply needs to scan the barcode and the coins will be transferred.

The bad news is that the list of companies, especially major companies, that accept these coins is still pretty small. The good news is that as more people start to use these currencies, and the more prevalent these currencies become, the more likely it is that companies will start joining this list.

Where Do I Store These Currencies?

Unlike fiat currency, you are not able to print off these currencies and take them to the store with you. You will not be able to store them in your physical wallet and then use them how you want. So, how are you supposed to use these currencies to make payments?

There are online wallets that you can use that will store these currencies for you. There are many different options that you can choose from based on the features that you want and how much security is necessary.

If you sign up with an exchange site, you will receive an online wallet from the site. This option works well if you plan to use the currencies right away. If you plan on investing those coins, it is better to pick out one of the other types of wallets to keep the coins more secure.

There are a few types of wallets that you can use for this. Some of the different wallet types that you can choose from include:

Online wallet: These wallets are completely online. They are convenient to use because the coins are already right where you need them and you can access the coins from any system. These are more susceptible to hacking attacks so your coins may not be as secure with them.

Hardware wallet: These wallets adds a bit more security to your coin storage because you take them offline and place the coins on your computer or a USB drive. This adds a few steps to using the coins but can add in some of the security that investors need.

Cold storage. These are the most secure because you are taking the coins completely off your computer and printing off the private key. It will add more steps to the process, but for long-term investments, it is the best option for safety.

The Benefits of Cryptocurrencies Over Fiat Currencies

There are quite a few benefits that you will be able to receive when it comes to using cryptocurrencies instead of your traditional fiat currency. These benefits include:

- Easy to join as long as you have an internet connection
- Able to maintain your privacy
- Transactions can be done instantly
- Low transaction fees when transferring money to others in different countries
- No central authority controlling how the currency works
- Many options on currencies to use
- A great investment option

The Negatives of Cryptocurrencies Over Fiat Currencies

While there are a lot of benefits to using these cryptocurrencies, there are also a few risks that you need to be aware of. These risks can make it hard to decide whether to get into the market or not. Some of the risks that you may face with these currencies include:

- High volatility that will change the value of the currency from one day to the next
- No guarantee of having your money if the value goes way down
- If the currency fails, you lose out on everything
- Investing can be risky with all the highs and lows
- Lots of scammers to watch out for when joining
- Hackers often try to get onto the network and steal your coins.

Main Options for Cryptocurrencies

As we mentioned before, there are a variety of cryptocurrencies that you can choose from. It often depends on what you are hoping to get out of your currency whether it is a good choice for you or not. Some of the major players right now in the cryptocurrency market include:

Bitcoin: Bitcoin has the advantage of being the first cryptocurrency released. It is the most recognized and the one that is most widely accepted. Right now the market cap of Bitcoin is estimated to be around $80 billion, and the value is currently at $11,000, even though it has seen a higher value than this throughout the past few months. Bitcoin is easily accessible with many merchants and exchanges available to use, it has more liquidity compared to other cryptocurrencies, and it has had time to prove that its security is in place. This is definitely a good place to start when looking for a cryptocurrency to work with.

Bitcoin Cash: Bitcoin Cash is a split off from Bitcoin. Many people were worried about how the original Bitcoin would be able to react as it grew and more people joined the network. They thought the transactions would be too slow and that there needed to be more coins available. This is when Bitcoin Cash came into existence. Those who already owned Bitcoin could choose to stay with that company and continue using their coins on that network, or they could easily exchange their coins over and join the Bitcoin Cash network.

Ethereum: Ethereum is another digital currency you can use. It is slightly different than other cryptocurrencies. This one is more of a platform that helps developers create their own applications without censorship, fraud, or any interference from other parties. Right now, the market cap of Ethereum is above $29 billion, and the price is $300 (up from $8 at the beginning of 2017). This currency is often overshadowed by Bitcoin, but it is a very safe and secure investment opportunity.

Ripple: Ripple is a network that you can use to send and receive money to anyone in the world. It works well for sending and receiving various fiat currencies, but you can also send over cryptocurrencies like Bitcoin and Ethereum if you would like.

Litecoin: this is an internet currency that will allow the user to send instant payments at low cost to anyone they want to in the world. It is a global network of payment that has become decentralized, so you don't have to worry about someone being around and messing with your money. Litecoin is known for faster transaction times, and it is more efficient at storing information compared to some of the other cryptocurrencies out there. With a lot of support, large trade volume, and a good amount of liquidity, you will find that Litecoin can be a great option for your investment.

These are just a few of the options that you can choose from when it is time to pick out a cryptocurrency. It is important that you do your research and figure out which one will be the right one for you. There are a lot of choices in the cryptocurrency world, but not all of them are legitimate options, and many will end up failing soon. Picking the wrong one can lead you into the hands of scammers or make it so your coins become worthless before you can use them.

As you can see, there are many different aspects of the cryptocurrency market. There are options to choose from, though, which can make the market even more fun to join.

Chapter 2: What is the Blockchain?

One of the most important parts behind Bitcoin and the other cryptocurrencies on the market is the blockchain. Without the blockchain technology, it would be impossible for these currencies to do well. The blockchain helps to provide both the transparency and the security that these currencies need to attract new users to them. Without having a central authority around to provide these, it is sometimes hard to convince users that their money is safe when it is only available online. The blockchain is the main reason that we can trust this kind of technology in the first place.

The blockchain is basically a secure ledger that can hold onto anything of value. In the case of cryptocurrencies, it will hold onto information about all of your transactions. You will have your own personal blockchain while on the network, and it will be added to the main blockchain for the network. You can look through both of these at any time that you would like.

Think of this like your bank statement. You will receive chains that hold onto your daily transactions with the cryptocurrency. These are similar to your monthly bank account statements. The blockchain will hold all of these chains together, such as your permanent record at the bank. You can always go through and look at these transactions to make sure they match up, and everything is in place.

In addition to being able to hold onto all your transactions, the blockchain technology is also fast. When you are working with your traditional bank to complete transactions, it can take a minimum of a few days to complete the transactions. This can be really frustrating when we are working in the modern world of getting things done instantly.

When you work with the blockchain though, you can get the transactions done almost instantly. The type of blockchain that you work with will often determine how fast the currencies are taken care of, but they are all under ten minutes. This is much faster than the several days that you see with your regular bank.

This works because the blockchain is one ledger. Everyone who joins the network will use the same blockchain, so things only need to be reconciled in one place. When you work with your bank though, the transaction needs to be reconciled both at your chosen bank as well as at the bank of the one that you are sending the money to. This can really slow things down when you send money traditionally.

Another benefit is that this blockchain ledger is pretty secure. Not only will it hold onto all the information about your transactions, but it will also prevent others from getting onto the ledger and fudging numbers or hiding information. This is something that traditional banks have suffered from in recent years and has taken away some of the trustworthiness that they used to have. The blockchain, on the other hand, has put in a few security features to prevent this from happening.

Whenever a new chain is added to the main blockchain, which will happen when a user fills it up, it will be given a unique code. There are various requirements for this code, but the most important one is that the characters need to be dependent on each other. This means that if even one character is changed, it will change all the characters that come after it in the code as well.

Not only that, but the characters also need to match up with the rest of the blockchain, ensuring that if anything in the whole blockchain is changed, it will change up everything. This takes some time to come up with the right codes but makes it easier for anyone to see if the chain is being messed with.

For most of the users of a cryptocurrency, how the blockchain works is not so important, and you will never spend time working on these codes. Miners are the ones who will take the time to complete these codes, and they are usually rewarded by the network when they are done. It is a good way for some people to make money while helping to keep the network secure.

How the Blockchain Works

While the technology behind blockchain is complex, the way that it works is simple. Whenever you join the network for a cryptocurrency that is based on the blockchain, you will receive a chain of your own to use. You don't need to do anything extra for this to happen as the network will just send it over.

As you work on your transactions, they will be added to your chain. You can look at the chain and see information about the money that people send to you, the purchases that you make, and any other exchange that you are doing on the network. These chains are set up to hold onto any transaction that you complete on that cryptocurrency network. They are also set up to hold a predetermined amount of transactions. Some people will fill them up quickly, and others may take more time depending on how busy they are on the network.

Once a particular chain is filled up, it will join the blockchain. As a user on this network, you will have your own personal blockchain, one that only has your transaction history present on it. In addition, after the miners have done their job and added a unique code to your chain, it will be added to the permanent blockchain for that network.

As you finish up with one chain, the network will automatically send you over another chain to use. You will not need to request this or do anything else to receive this chain. This process will continue on for as long as you are using the network. The more transactions that you complete and the longer you are on the network, the longer your blockchain will be.

How the Miners Come Into Play

One important part of the blockchain is the work that the miners do. Without the miners, it would be impossible to maintain the security and safety that is so important on this network.

With the blockchain, it is set up to add some transparency. This happens because anyone on the network can look through the transactions and ensure that everything is legitimate. However, you don't want everyone to just look at the blockchain and be able to steal all your personal information.

The work of the miners is to help hide your personal information in the transactions so that it is still present, but a hacker or someone else can't see it all. When they complete their job, it will also be easy for any user to tell if someone has been trying to make unauthorized changes to the blockchain.

A miner will get the right equipment to solve complex mathematical equations. The point of this is to help them create a new code that goes with each chain on the blockchain. Creating these codes are not easy and the longer the cryptocurrency is on the market, the harder it is to create these codes.

These codes need to have a level of difficulty to them. Otherwise, everyone would jump on the process and al the codes would be done in no time. In addition, all the coins will disappear since these are given out as a reward.

There are a number of requirements that come with creating these codes. First, the need to be unique and can't match the code that is on any of the other parts of the blockchain. In addition, each character needs to be tied to the other characters, both in the individual chains and in the whole blockchain.

What this means is that if any one character is changed, then it will change all the characters that proceed it. This makes it more difficult to create the codes, but it also ensures that no one can make changes to the code after it is completed. If someone tries to change up the code, you will see a big mess show up on the blockchain.

Many miners will choose to use some mining software to help them create these codes. This software can help to speed up the process, but there is a lot of competition in the mining market. Mining can be difficult, but the reward that these currencies provide makes it a lucrative way to make some money.

There are a few things that a miner needs to be a good miner. Some of these include:

- A dedicated computer for mining
- A dedicated spot to do the mining process in, preferably someplace that is cool.
- Mining software
- A good graphics card to take care of the work.

- A wallet to hold your earnings
- An interest and curiosity to work in mining.

With all the work that comes with the mining process, you may wonder why anyone would want to get into this process. The mining process is hard, but those who are successful will be able to earn a profit. The network will release some coins to the winner, and they can use them however they would like.

The reward that you are offered will vary based on which cryptocurrency you are working with. For example, Bitcoin will provide 25 coins each time that you complete a code. Most other currencies don't offer this high of a reward, but at this point, Bitcoin is one of the most difficult currencies to mine.

The mining process is important when it comes to the cryptocurrency market. It helps to keep the market safe, helps to release more coins into the market, and allows the miners to earn a nice profit for their work.

Ways the Blockchain Can Be Used

The most well-known way that blockchain can be used is with cryptocurrencies. But while the blockchain technology was released at the same time as Bitcoin, there are actually quite a few other ways that this technology can be used. And with the beginning of Ethereum, there are now more developers than ever who are looking to create their own blockchain platform. This makes it easier to bring blockchain into the future.

There are so many ways that blockchain technology can be used. Some of these methods include:

- Voting and elections
- Speeding up transactions at banks
- Insurance policies
- Hotel reservations
- Polling
- Car reservations

- Smart contracts that eliminate the need for a third party in negotiations
- And more!

Without the blockchain, it is unlikely that we would be talking about cryptocurrencies and how great they are. This technology allows users to feel that their information is safe and that all transactions are accounted for, even though everything is online. While the blockchain can be used for a variety of other purposes as well, it was first introduced as a way to help keep Bitcoin, and other cryptocurrencies safe and it has done a great job at accomplishing this goal.

Chapter 3: The Beginnings of Cryptocurrency

There have been attempts for a digital currency ever since the 1990s when the tech boom went on. Some options, like DigiCash, Beenz, and Flooz came out on the market, but they were never able to gain traction, and they soon failed. There were various reasons why all of these failed, including financial problems, issues between employees at a company, and even fraud.

One thing that all of those digital currencies shared is that they utilized an approach that relied on a trusted third party. What this means is that the companies that designed these currencies were there to verify and facilitate the transactions. Since the companies ended up failing, the creation of a cash system that was completely digital was seen as a lost cause for quite some time.

In 2009, things began to change. Under the alias of Satoshi Nakamoto, an anonymous group introduced what is now known as Bitcoin. It was described as a peer-to-peer electronic cash system. This system was completely decentralized, which means that there isn't a central authority or any servers that are in control over the currency. A good way to describe this is that the concept resembles peer-to-peer networks for file sharing.

One of the problems that this new currency needed to solve was the issue of double-spending. With this issue, you have to worry about the technique of fraudulently spending the same amount twice. Traditionally, companies would use a trusted third-party to help prevent this issue. However, this means that a central authority would need to control all your funds and your personal details. This was something that the new online currency wanted to avoid.

With a network that is decentralized like Bitcoin, it is up to all the participants to do this job. This is done through the blockchain, a public ledger that holds onto all the transactions that ever occur on the network. Everyone can look over the transactions whenever they would like to ensure that all transactions are in place.

With Bitcoin, the idea was to allow people to have a way to send and receive money without a central authority controlling it. Many users of this network liked this idea because they didn't have to worry about a government getting into the middle of the currency and messing things up. Instead, everything that happens on the Bitcoin network is controlled by a mathematical equation.

For example, there are only so many coins that were created with Bitcoin; 21 million. And not all of these coins were released at the same time. These coins are slowly released as miners complete their job of protecting information found on the blockchain. This helps to slowly introduce more coins to the market while keeping a central authority out of the process.

The blockchain technology is critical in helping to keep this network as safe as possible. This ledger is responsible for holding onto all the transactions that occur on the Bitcoin network. You can even use it to send and receive money to anywhere throughout the world.

While Bitcoin was one of the first cryptocurrencies to make it on the market successfully, there are now many more. It is estimated that there are more than 1000 cryptocurrencies available. Not all of them will stick around for a long time, and most will disappear within a few months of being started. But there are still many big names in the game.

In addition to Bitcoin, you can find names such as Dogecoin, Litecoin, Bitcoin Cash, Ripple, Ethereum, and many more. These are great ones to use based on what you need the currency for. For example, Bitcoin is a great option to go with if you are looking for an online payment method, Ripple is a good option for sending payments to others across the world, and Ethereum is good for those who would like to work with developing the blockchain technology.

Each currency has its place in the market, and if they have successfully come up with a niche to work with, they are likely to stick around for a long time to come. Some will fail, but those with good security, the ability to keep information private, and a good blockchain, are sure to be around for some time.

Chapter 4: How to Get Started in Cryptocurrencies

Getting started in cryptocurrencies is a simple process. You will need to go through a few steps to make it happen, but it is not set up to be difficult or hard to do. This is one of the many reasons that so many people throughout the world have decided to join one of the many cryptocurrency networks. As long as you have access to the internet and you can exchange some fiat money for cryptocurrency, you can get started. If you participate in the mining process or are a business that accepts these cryptocurrencies, you don't even need to worry about exchanging money to get started.

The first step that you need to take is to find an exchange site. There are several of these available to choose from but do your research ahead of time. With the start of the cryptocurrency boom, there are a lot of legitimate exchange sites out there, but there are also a lot of scammers out there. If you are not careful, it is possible to give your money to an exchange site and never see a dime of the cryptocurrency you desire.

One of the best exchange sites that you can go with in the United States is Coinbase. This one accepts Bitcoin, Ethereum, and Litecoin exchanges right now, with talks to take on a few of the other big ones sometime in the near future. This exchange site works well, is secure, and will only take a few steps for you to get signed up.

To start, you need to visit www.coinbase.com. From here, you can go through the steps, providing a little bit of personal information to open up your account. Right now the amount of information you need to provide is minimal, but this may change in the future. The United States government is working on regulations that would require these exchange sites to collect more information in the hopes of reducing issues like money laundering. This takes away from the anonymity that most people want with cryptocurrencies, but is not an issue right now.

After providing your information, you will need to complete a phone verification before the account can be opened. At this point, you are ready to proceed to your dashboard and look around.

At the dashboard, you will be able to see which accounts are available through Coinbase, the current exchange rate of these currencies, and even what accounts you have set up. If you would like to exchange your fiat currency for the chosen cryptocurrency, you will need to set up a payment method to make this happen.

There are three main methods that you can use on Coinbase to exchange your coins. You can choose to use your bank account, a credit or debit card, or your PayPal account. Each of these can have their own benefits and negatives to choose the one that is best for your needs.

The first option is to use your bank account. Setting up a bank account does not have to be difficult, but it will take some extra time. Since you are working with a financial institution, it can take about three to five days to transfer the money over. For those who want to get investing quickly in these markets, the bank account may not be the best option. If, on the other hand, you would like to invest a larger amount of money, then the bank account option is a good one to choose.

Many people like to work with either their credit and debit cards or with their PayPal account. These options are much faster. They can get the money over to their account very quickly, making them the best option if you are looking to get into day trading or one of the other similar options. However, your credit limit (or the amount that you can transfer at once), is much lower with one of these two options.

Some people choose to use more than one option to help increase how much they can invest in the market. You will need to go through and complete the verification process for each one, but you can link up as many accounts as you would like.

Once you have linked up your chosen account, you can exchange out the fiat currency for the cryptocurrency. Take a look at the exchange rate before you do this to ensure that you know how much you are getting out of the process. Coinbase will walk you through the other steps that you need and then will send the coins to your online wallet.

Coinbase provides you with a unique wallet through its exchange site. If you plan to use the coins right away, it is fine to use that wallet. Keep in mind that many online wallets are not considered the most secure from hackers. And with the Coinbase wallet, your address will include your first and last name, which makes it easier for others to track your transactions.

If you are planning on investing your coins, or you would like to add some more security to your currency, there are other wallets that you can choose. There are online wallets that make it easy to use the coins right away. There are also hardware wallets and cold storage wallets that help you to hide the coins from hackers and keep them safe. You can choose the wallet that you like based on how secure you want the coins and the features that they offer.

From this point, you can use the coins as you would like. You can use them to make purchases, send money to other people, or even exchange them back out for your fiat currency after you have invested for some time. There are so many options that come with investing in these cryptocurrencies and once you have your Coinbase account, or you have set yourself up through another exchange site, it is easy to join the network and get things done.

Chapter 5: Will Society Accept These Cryptocurrencies?

The biggest issue with cryptocurrencies is whether society will accept these currencies and be willing to work with them. Traditionally, we are used to working with fiat money, money that is secured and ran by the federal government or another big government agency.

We may not always agree with the way that the government is running things at time, but we like the security this system brings. If something happens to our money, or even if the bank that holds our money fails, we know that our money is backed by the government and we won't lose everything.

Cryptocurrencies are a bit different. They do not rely on any entity to control them. Rather, they are set up to run based on a mathematical equation. Everything happens online, and the users are the ones in charge of making sure the system will stay safe. Is this enough to help users feel safe and secure using these online currencies?

It seems that society is welcoming these cryptocurrencies will open arms. Bitcoin aloe was worth over $18,000 a coin at one point. People all over the world accept these coins and even some major businesses are now accepting Bitcoin and other cryptocurrencies as a form of payment. And thanks to the security that the blockchain technology adds to the system, users can complete their transactions while keeping their information safe.

So, how do users learn how to trust this system? These are the first of their kind and have only been around for a short time. There isn't anyone to protect the money either if something goes wrong. Why would you want to choose to put your money into these currencies in the first place?

There are actually many great benefits that come with using these cryptocurrencies, and this is why so many people throughout the world have chosen to use them on a daily basis to send and receive money. Some of the benefits of working with cryptocurrencies include:

Easy to use: These cryptocurrencies are pretty easy to work with. You need to set up a wallet to hold onto the coins that you are using. You need to sign up with the network to get a unique address that will be used each time that you complete a transaction on the network. And you need to exchange out your fiat currency for the cryptocurrency of your choice. All of these only take a few minutes to complete, making this one of the easiest things to join.

Available all throughout the world: As long as you can get online and the ability to exchange some of your fiat money for the cryptocurrency of your choice, you can join one of these networks and get started! You can choose to send and receive money or even to invest to put your money to work for you. There is something for everyone when it comes to working with cryptocurrencies.

A good investment: Many people get into cryptocurrencies because they are a great tool for investing. There are many options you can go with for investing, from the strategy that you use to which coins will provide the best return on investment.

Uses the blockchain technology: The blockchain technology is really amazing and can do so much for keeping information safe on the cryptocurrency network. It can get transactions done within a few minutes. It can ensure that you can keep your personal information private. It shows transparency in the network because everyone can look at the ledger and make sure the information is correct. And it can even limit the amount that you pay in transaction fees. Without this great blockchain technology, it is unlikely that these cryptocurrencies would be doing as well as they are.

Keeps your information private: It is possible to keep your personal information private when working with cryptocurrencies. You get the benefit of picking out your own unique address to work with. And thanks to the work the miners do on the blockchain, all the information about our transactions can stay private as well. Pick out a good wallet as well so you can complete all the transactions you would like without others stealing your personal information.

Quick transactions: When you send money for a payment through your bank or credit card, the transaction time can take three to five days. This is a long time considering our instant and online world. With the help of the blockchain technology, you will be able to send payments within a few minutes, rather than waiting a few days.

Low transaction fees: If you have ever sent money to someone else through your bank, especially if that person is located in another country, you know how quickly those transaction fees can add up. If you need to do this on a regular basis, it will be expensive. When you send money through a cryptocurrency though, you will be able to do this without all the high transaction fees involved.

While the idea behind these cryptocurrencies are brand-new and not something we have seen before, they are really taking the world by storm. Society has accepted them, and many people are now using them. Whether these currencies are being used for sending money, receiving money, or for investing, they have been accepted and are here to stay.

Chapter 6: What Setbacks Have Occurred with Cryptocurrencies?

There are so many things that you can enjoy when you work with a cryptocurrency. You can complete payments without a third-party interfering. You can lower your risks of doing things online. It can be used by anyone in the world. And you can keep your privacy when it comes to sending and receiving money online.

However, these cryptocurrencies are new, and they are still getting some of the kinks worked out. This means that there will be some setbacks that they need to work out before these coins can become universally accepted. Some of these setbacks are not that important and were fixed quickly. Others are a big deal that, without being properly dealt with, could have been a big blow to how well these currencies are accepted. Let's take a look at some of the setbacks and flaws that have already shown up with cryptocurrencies.

Users Don't Properly Understand Cryptocurrencies

While the world of cryptocurrencies, such as Bitcoin, are growing, there are still a lot of people who know nothing about cryptocurrency or about the digital currency world. This is similar to what happened when credit cards were announced. Many people now own several credit cards and use them on a regular basis, but when they were first introduced, people thought it was impossible to pay for things using a card.

The same issue is found with digital currencies. Some people, even if they have heard about cryptocurrencies, are finding it difficult to understand that they can use these currencies to send and receive money. Digital currencies are different, and they don't involve any cash, which makes some people doubt whether they are really effective for making purchases.

To make these cryptocurrencies more acceptable, it is important for more people to be educated about these currencies so they can learn how to include them in their daily lives. A good way to do this is through networking. This is a slow process though, and it will take some time before more users are willing to get into the market and use these coins on a regular basis. As they learn more about these currencies and see more businesses accept these currencies, the setback will start to go away.

Lack Of Any Guarantee And Protection

Some people do not like the idea of having a government control their money. They want to have some freedom with their money and not have to worry about how the government is messing with inflation and other things concerning their money.

This is a problem that cryptocurrencies can solve. However, there is an issue with no protection on these networks. Since there isn't a central authority controlling these online currencies, there is no protection if something goes wrong.

If a hacker gets into your wallet and takes your coins, you are out of luck unless you have a backup of the private key. If there is a computer glitch and you lose your coins, you have now lost all your coins. If the currency ends up failing and becomes worthless overnight, then you have lost all of your money. In all of these cases, you will lose your money, and no one is there to help you out.

Technical Shortcomings

If there ends up being an issue with one of your transactions because of a technical glitch in the system, where are you supposed to turn? There isn't a bank you can call up and talk to about this issue. While the blockchain has done a good job keeping transactions in their place, there is always the issue of a technical mix up, and then you lose out on all your money in the process.

Hackers Getting Into the System

There are a few cryptocurrencies, such as Ethereum, that have had problems with keeping their security in place. They have been attacked by hackers. These hackers have been able to get onto the network and steal coins right out of the wallets of those on the network.

While Ethereum and some of the others have upped their security to prevent this issue from occurring, it is still an issue that a lot of users need to consider. What are you going to do if you open your wallet one day and all the coins are gone? With many people using these cryptocurrencies as a form of investment, this could be a big risk to your profit.

These are some of the most common setbacks that cryptocurrencies have faced over the past few years. Many of these currencies have developers who are working to fix these issues, but without some of the support that traditional banking methods have, there is still an element of risk to using cryptocurrencies.

Chapter 7: The Different Types of Cryptocurrencies

Each cryptocurrency that you come across has some major differences. Some are meant to be payment methods, some are ways to send money, and some work to help expand the work that the blockchain can do. Each of the successful ones is meant to fill in a niche so that people will use them and keep them around.

One of the most fundamental technical differences between the cryptocurrencies is the algorithms that are employed. Some currencies, like Bitcoin, will use the SHA-256 algorithm, while others, like Litecoin, will use a newer algorithm that is known as Scrypt.

There are a few significant changes that these currencies can bring to the table. The main significance of these algorithms is how they impact the mining of new coins. With all of these digital currencies, confirming a transaction will require a lot of computer power. Some members of the currency network, who are called miners, will use their own resources to completing this task for the users. They are then rewarded with units of that currency when they are successful.

For the most part, SHA-256 is considered the more complex algorithm when compared to Scrypt. It also allows for more parallel processing. Miners who use this kind of algorithm will need to use more sophisticated forms of mining to be as efficient as possible.

For example, when it comes to mining Bitcoin, most miners use Application-Specific Integrated Circuits, also known as ASICs. These can be tailored made to only mine Bitcoins. The consequence of the ASIC is that it has made it almost impossible for the everyday user to mine Bitcoin.

On the other hand, Scrypt was designed to be less susceptible to the custom hardware solutions that are used in ASIC-based mining. These cryptocurrencies and the mining process that runs them are more accessible to users who want to work as miners.

In addition, working with a Scrypt currency usually means that the transaction will be completed faster. SHA-256 may have been the first introduced on the market, but it averages about nine minutes to add the transaction to the main ledger. On the other hand, Scrypt currencies can do this in less than three minutes.

Both of these types of currencies are popular and have made their way onto the cryptocurrency scene. But some of the ones that are employing Scrypt, such as Litecoin, are gaining in popularity because of the speed that they bring to the table. Since they are newer, they have also had time to work out some of the bugs that the older currencies have dealt with, allowing them to be faster, safer, and easier to use.

More Differences Between Cryptocurrencies

While the background of these cryptocurrencies, such as whether they are ran with scrypt or the blockchain, is one of the biggest differences between many cryptocurrencies, other differences are important as well. Let's take a look at some more information about the differences that can occur between the various cryptocurrencies.

Differences in online currencies

Any currency that doesn't have a physical representation and resides on a set of computer systems is known as a digital currency. These have actually been around for more than twenty years, and the whole purpose is to enable online purchases.

One type of digital currency is known as a virtual currency. These are digital currencies that are unregulated and are often used by one specific online community. This could include a coin that is used inside a mobile game to make in-app purchases. The coins would have no purpose outside of making purchases in that app.

However, if the virtual currency is then used to as a medium of exchange, and it uses cryptography to secure the transactions, it turns into a cryptocurrency. Bitcoin is one of the best-known examples of a cryptocurrency.

Categorizing a coin or a token

There are also some differences in whether the cryptocurrency can be counted as a coin or a token. If a cryptocurrency can operate on its own, has its own unique rules, its own blockchain, and its own governance structure, it will be known as a coin.

The coin is like an incentive that will be used to reward the participants in the network. For example, Bitcoin and Litecoin will reward a miner with these coins based on the completion of a successful code.

On the other hand, if the cryptocurrency depends on the blockchain network or the platform of another cryptocurrency to operate, it will be known as a token. Each transaction that happens on the token is also going to be considered a transaction on the parent platform, but the parent platform will still have its own currency.

There are several examples of these tokens. BAT, TenX, and OmiseGo are all tokens that use the Ethereum network to work properly. However, Ethereum uses its own coin, known as the Ether, to keep running.

Categorizing non-Bitcoin cryptocurrencies

When you hear about altcoin, you may be curious what this means. An altcoin is any cryptocurrency that is not Bitcoin. Even if a currency forked off from Bitcoin and then became its own network, it will be an altcoin. An example of this would be Bitcoin Cash.

In addition, cryptocurrencies that are completely separate from Bitcoin and were never connected are considered as altcoins as well. Ethereum, Litecoin, and ZCash are examples of altcoins.

You can also work with colored coins or meta-coins. These are coins that will leverage the infrastructure of an existing coin, which helps them to enhance the features of that code. But these coins are never going to modify the source code of the original currency.

A good example of this is known as zerocoin. This was developed to add some privacy features to Bitcoins. Since these types of coins are used to create custom tokens on top of colored coins, which is why they are sometimes known as second layer cryptocurrencies.

The biggest issue with using these second layer cryptocurrencies is that they may have a problem knowing which blockchain to follow if there is ever a fork.

The mineability of a coin

For many cryptocurrencies, it is hard for them to run without the help of a miner. Miners are on what is known as the supply side of the market, and this puts some downward pressure on the price to prevent inflation. Some of the big names in the market, such as Dogecoin, Siacoin, and Bitcoin are all examples of a cryptocurrency that can be mined.

There are a few cryptocurrencies that are pre-mined, even though this is not that prevalent. What this means is that the entire supply of available coins will be generated with the first block of the blockchain. When this happens, all the coins will be owned by the company who designed that currency. This has happened, such as in the case of Ripple pre-mining 100 billion of their coins.

You will find that most meta-coins and tokens are non-mineable currencies. Miners may be able to go through and mine the coins in the parent network, but they will not be able to mine specifically for the tokens. This means that the tokens will become stores of value since they have a fixed supply.

Working with cryptocurrencies can be a fun experience. They allow you to learn more about the market and how it will grow in the future. However, some major differences occur in the various cryptocurrencies that will determine whether you will make a profit in them and whether they will stick around.

There are some good examples of all kinds of coins and tokens, but you must understand what you are getting yourself into before you get started. You can pick out a cryptocurrency to work with based on which factors they have similar, or you can look at a fundamental analysis to pick the right one for you.

Chapter 8: Will One Cryptocurrency Rule Them All?

Because there are so many people who are interested in trying out cryptocurrencies, the market for these currencies is quickly expanding. Many different cryptocurrencies are on the market. While Bitcoin was the first successful cryptocurrency, being released in 2009, there are now more than 1000 cryptocurrencies available on the market.

Most of these currencies are not going to stick around for the long-term. They came about because of the popularity of cryptocurrencies right now, not because they have the power to stay around. However, there are some cryptocurrencies, the ones that fit a specific niche or need, that are likely to be around for some time to come.

If one cryptocurrency will rule them all, it will be Bitcoin. Bitcoin was one of the first of these currencies to come on the market, and it has gained the most popularity. When you look up information about cryptocurrencies, the first thing you will find is about Bitcoin. If you ask anyone if they have ever heard about cryptocurrencies, it is likely they will talk about Bitcoin. Bitcoin has the largest market cap, has many different exchanges you can work with and is available throughout the world.

Some other cryptocurrencies are likely to stay around in the future as well. These digital currencies often focus on other aspects of the digital world rather than as a payment method. Bitcoin is the main event when it comes to an online payment method, and other digital currencies will have a hard time competing with this in the future.

However, other cryptocurrencies work in different niches. Ethereum, despite running into some security issues when it first started, is becoming a big name. This one is not a payment method though. It is more of a platform that is meant to help expand the blockchain technology. Investors and developers will come together on this network to make new blockchain applications and help it to grow.

Ripple is another big name that is likely to be around for some time. This is a safe and fast way to send money to anyone in the world. You can send any currency you would like, even Bitcoin and Ethereum, without as many fees or regulations as some of the other ones.

These three are the big names in the industry right now, though there are some other choices like Litecoin, Bitcoin Cash, and more. But if there is to be one digital currency that rules them all in the future, it is likely to be Bitcoin, the original cryptocurrency. The value of Bitcoin will settle down in the next few years, but it will still hold the biggest market cap and be the cryptocurrency that beginners and experts alike flock to.

Chapter 9: The Future of Bitcoin and the Blockchain Technology

The world of finances is changing rapidly. People are more likely to shop online than ever before, and they want easy and fast ways to send money to anyone around the world. They are tired of having to worry about how the government will mess with their money, tired of the high fees that their bank charges, and tired of the transaction delays that last three to five days any time they transfer money.

Cryptocurrencies like Bitcoin are a great solution to these complaints. While they may be in a bubble that prematurely raises the prices, it is likely that within the next few years, this will settle down. This doesn't mean that cryptocurrencies will be gone in the near future. It simply means that their values will settle down and some of the volatility will go out.

There are many reasons why cryptocurrencies, such as Bitcoin and Ethereum, are so popular and why they are likely to stick around in the future. These reasons include:

- Low transaction fees
- Use of the blockchain ledger to keep information safe
- Easy to use
- Send and receive money instantly
- Easier to hide personal information while shopping online
- No central authority controlling the money
- Can be used by anyone throughout the world
- Easy to invest in and make money from.

More than that, the blockchain technology is really going to propel industries into the future. There are so many industries that could provide better customer service if they were able to use this blockchain technology. Any business that handles anything of value could work with blockchain to keep track of information and more.

The banking industry is the biggest sector that would benefit from this technology since they deal with transactions just like in Bitcoin. With the blockchain ledger, transactions could be completed within a few minutes, rather than taking the traditional three to five days. Customer information would stay secure, making it harder for hackers to gain this information. Transaction fees would go way down. All these benefits and more are why many major banks, including a few in Europe who have banded together, are looking to develop their own blockchain technology.

While it may seem that the value of Bitcoin has been overinflated, it is not likely that this cryptocurrency will disappear. It solves so many solutions for its users and can easily adapt to our changing financial world. It is likely that the value of Bitcoin will steady out, and the volatility will go down, but the use of Bitcoin is likely to grow. And with all the uses of the blockchain ledger, it is likely that we will become very familiar with this kind of technology as the years go on.

The Future of Blockchain

There are a lot of people who are still not convinced that cryptocurrencies are here to stay. They feel that these currencies are not worth your time and that those who try to follow them will end up losing out on all of their money.

On the other side of things, many people feel that cryptocurrency is the way of the future. They feel that it won't be long before everyone decides that it is in their best interests to work with these cryptocurrencies and that these will take over the financial world.

There is no shortage of strong opinions about these digital currencies, especially when it comes to Bitcoin.

For example, Peter Thiel, the PayPal co-founder, predicts that Bitcoin will be around for some time and it will change the world as a currency. However, he doesn't see Bitcoin making it as much as a payment network, just that some of the technology behind it will make major changes.

Mark Cuban, on the other hand, has given Bitcoin the green-light. He sees Bitcoin as a viable digital accounting transport mechanism, but he also thinks that in the long-term cryptocurrency, he believes that there are better options that will eventually take over.

Bill Gates has even chimed in on this debate. He acknowledges that Bitcoin has essentially revolutionized how transactions can happen across-borders, but in its current state, it won't be the Money 2.0.

Warren Buffet has taken a look at Bitcoin as well and is giving the currency even less credit than all the others. He believes that the idea of cryptocurrency is like geek's gold and it is a big joke.

Regardless of what the specialists say about this currency, Bitcoin is not something to joke about. There are more and more entrepreneurs around the world who are taking a look at Bitcoin and even risking it all to invest in this currency. Just the fact that there are so many big names that have left their opinions about this currency shows that it has taken its place in the financial world. It may have to undergo some changes to make it in the future, but it looks like it is here to stay.

There are a lot of things that can happen with cryptocurrencies such as Bitcoin into the future. First, it will depend on how they adapt. There have already been a few issues that come up with Bitcoin, and it has had to change. For example, there have been issues with how fast transactions can be done on the Bitcoin network. The transactions take about ten minutes to be done on Bitcoin. While this is much faster than what happens in the financial world and in banks, it is much slower than what other cryptocurrencies can do. This can put Bitcoin behind some of the others until the problem is fixed.

There have also been some issues with how Bitcoin will run and whether the coins released are enough. Some of the fundamentals of Bitcoin have been challenged already, and the result is that there is now Bitcoin and Bitcoin Cash.

Bitcoin may be able to make it into the future, but it does need to make some major changes to keep up. There is a lot more competition in the cryptocurrency market than there was when Bitcoin was started. And many of those currencies are working to compete with Bitcoin and succeeding.
The way that governments react to these currencies will have a big determinant on how well they do in the future. Right now, some

countries promote these currencies, and this is where cryptocurrency is really growing strong. On the other hand, in some countries where there are more regulations and government interference, cryptocurrencies are not growing as quickly as they could.

These cryptocurrencies are sure to be around for a long time to come, and Bitcoin is leading the pack. These currencies are better able to adapt to the changing economy, much better than banks and other financial institutions have been able to do to this point.

While financial institutions still add on a lot of fees for their work, take three to five days to complete transactions, and make people jump through hoops to set up accounts, cryptocurrencies don't have these issues. They can complete the transactions for hardly any fees, can get the transactions done in a few minutes, and you can join as long as you sign up for an account and have a payment method to exchange.

And as time goes on, there are more and more cryptocurrencies that are changing and evolving the way that we do business in the financial world. The banking industry is taking notice and jumping on as well. Several of the major banks in Europe have joined together to create their own blockchain technology, taking their cues from the Bitcoin network, to help speed up transactions between them and to provide better customer service.

Some banks are even teaming up with Ripple to facilitate big payments in a matter of seconds. Ripple helps them to get this done without having to worry about reconciling things on two different ledgers, speeding up the process for the banks.

These are a few examples of how these cryptocurrencies are taking over the world. And they are still new. As time goes on, it is likely that these cryptocurrencies will continue to grow and adapt, allowing them to be used in the financial world more than ever before. Regardless of your opinion on Bitcoin and some of the other cryptocurrencies, they have already changed the financial landscape and will be here to change it more and more in the future.

Part 2: Understanding the Big 4

Chapter 1: Is This a Bubble?

The world of cryptocurrencies is growing, and news about these coins seems to be all over the place. It is hard to imagine that there are still a lot of people who have never even heard of this market. With all the current news about these currencies, it is no wonder that so many people are becoming excited about them, especially investors who are looking to make a quick profit.

The cryptocurrency market has grown like crazy. It is believed that these currencies have topped out with a market cap of $120 billion right now and many of the top currencies, such as Bitcoin, have reached record highs without signs of slowing down. Many people want to get into this hot market, whether it is to try out the currency, to send and receive money, or even to invest and earn a profit.

Even with all of this talk around cryptocurrencies, some analysists caution that being careful is the best way to treat these cryptocurrencies. They worry that these records gains are not sustainable and soon the cryptocurrency market will start going downhill quickly.

There is a lot of talk about how these cryptocurrencies are taking over in a big way, and this talk has even expanded to how these coins may even outpace cash in the near future. Still, many believe that the way these digital currencies are acting is representative of a bubble. Bubbles are worrisome, but not all bad

According to Clem Chambers, an analyst for Forbes, cryptocurrencies are a bubble over the short-term. This means that investors and users need to be careful about using these currencies. The huge increase in value of these coins over the past few months means that they are more likely to crash when the market is not able to hold these new values.

However, Chambers also argues that when looking at this market overall, the industry is likely to go up over the long-term, making it a good option for investors. Investors need to be willing to get into the market and ride out some of the bad times though. The market will go down before it goes back up and sticking it out can provide you with a huge profit.

So, why would you want to go with an investment that is likely to go down in the near future and hopefully will go back up? Take a look at the dotcom boom. There are some big companies, some of the biggest in the world, which became prevalent during this dotcom boom. While the dotcom bubble burst, similar to what is predicted with the cryptocurrency market, many of these big companies are still around and thriving.

Why Should I Consider Investing In Cryptocurrency?

So, it looks like the cryptocurrency market is likely to be a bubble right now. The huge increase in value of these coins makes it unlikely that they will be able to support that increase in the future. These currencies are likely to decrease in value, at least in the short-term, something that no investor wants to hear.

The good news is that while this bubble is likely to burst, it will clean up the market. Cryptocurrencies are really popular and have many benefits that people in the financial world have been looking for. They have some real value in the real world, especially since they work with blockchain, and it is unlikely that they will disappear completely.

What is likely to happen is that they will consolidate. Right now we are dealing with more than 1000 cryptocurrencies around the world. This is way too many. Most are just taking up room in the market, and many are even scams and worthless already.

When the bubble bursts, all of the coins will see a decrease in value. For some of the big names, they will lose money, but they will still have enough value to stick around. The smaller names, the ones with very little value to start with, are likely to fail and disappear completely.

With less competition in the market, the main cryptocurrencies will be able to rebound and go back up in value. The financial market has plenty of room for these digital currencies, but they will have to reform, and the market will need to change a bit for them to survive. This will happen when the cryptocurrency bubble pops.

The big names in cryptocurrency and the ones that have a good solid foundation are the ones that are likely to stick around, even after the bubble. A bubble may seem like a bad thing, but in reality, they allow the market to weed out the bad and keep around the good. And this is good news for all those investors.

As an investor, if you can get through this bubble, you will still stand to earn a lot of money. You must make sure that you are picking out a currency that will stick around, and you need to be prepared to go through this downturn. But cryptocurrencies are here to stay and will provide you with a good return on investment, even if some of them are likely to disappear.

Chapter 2: How to Pick a Good Cryptocurrency to Work with?

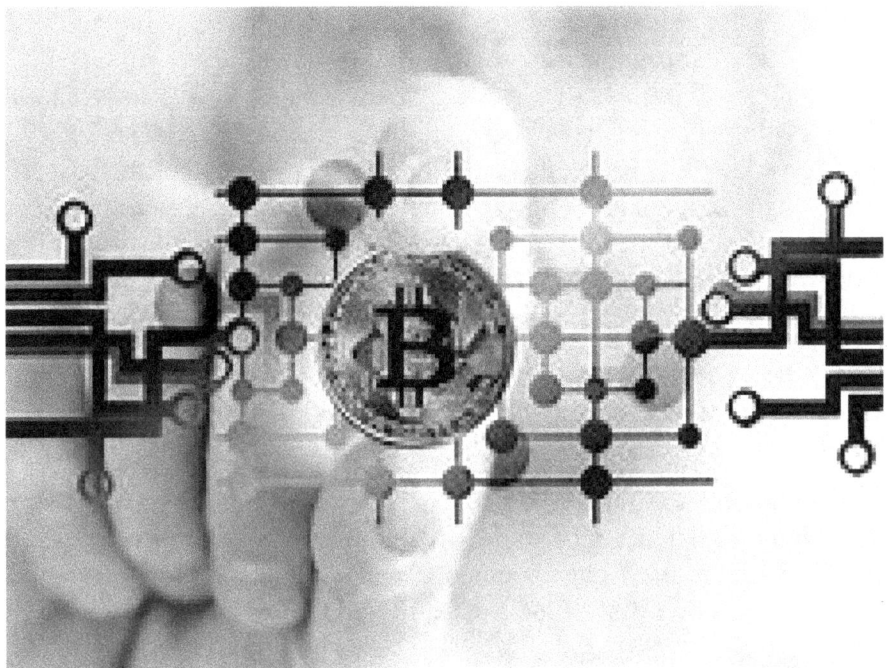

Now that you are ready to get started with your investment opportunity, it is important that you learn which currencies are the best for you to go with. There are a lot of cryptocurrencies that you can pick from, but not all of them will provide you with the return on investment that you want. When you are picking out a currency to invest in, take a look at some of these factors to help you out.

Good Market Cap

One of the first things that people will look at when they pick out which cryptocurrency to work with is the market cap. This is a good indicator of how well a currency is doing and how many users are on the network. As an investor, you want to make sure that you pick out a cryptocurrency with a decent market cap to ensure there is enough interested buyers and sellers to make the investment worth your time. Has the right security features behind it

While you are doing your research about a currency, make sure that you look at the security features that come with it. No user will stick with a currency that has a major hacking attack. They want to get onto the network and know that their information is safe and secure. If the currency is not able to guarantee that security, the users will leave and find a different currency.

Most cryptocurrencies have been safe from hacking attacks so far, although some, like Ethereum, have had issues with this in the past. If there is a hacking attack, your personal information, and your coins, are at risk. Even if the currency hasn't had issues with security attacks, look at what security protocols they have in place to keep your investment safe.

The Value of The Currency

Take some time to look at the value of a currency before you decide to invest in it. You don't need to go with a currency that has the highest value to make money, but you need to make sure that the coin is worth something and that the value has steadily gone up since it began.

No matter how new the currency is, there should be some information on how the coin has been doing. You want the currency to keep going up. It does not need to go up dramatically like Bitcoin has, but you should be able to see that there is a steady upward trend in the coin.

If you notice that the coin has a long period of time where its value does not increase, or you see that the currency seems to trend down more than up, it is not a good investment. For you to make money with a cryptocurrency, you need to see the value go up from your initial investment. So, if the currency is not going up, you will never make any money.

There will be times when the currency goes down. This has happened with all cryptocurrencies at some point. Some of these downward trends are temporary and will only last a few days, while others are more long-term and could indicate an issue with the currency.

The History of The Coin

Another thing that you can look at is the history of the cryptocurrency you want to work with. Those that have been around for a longer time are often good investments because they have gathered some followers and haven't had any major setbacks that turned the customers away.

This doesn't mean that you can't work with coins that are a little newer. The oldest coin has only been around since 2009 so none of them have a lot of history that you can work with. But no matter how new the coin is you can still take a look at how well it has been doing to help predict how well it will do in the future.

When looking at the history, look to see that the coin has had a steady amount of growth over that time. You can look to see if there have been any major downturns in the value of the currency and what caused these dips. You can look at some of the complaints with the currency, look to see if there are any security issues and more. Looking through this information can help you to see if the currency is a safe investment for you.

Look At the Business Model of the Coin

It is not enough to just look at the value of each coin to determine if it is a good investment. Some coins may be good at advertising and can get people to sign up in the beginning. This helps to inflate the value in the beginning and may make it look like a good investment. But without a good business model behind it, the users will disappear, and the value will go crashing.

It may seem kind of crazy that you need to see a business model to determine if a currency is worth your time, but you have to make sure the currency is legitimate, not one that will die out within a few weeks.

The business model doesn't have to be complex. Bitcoin was designed to be a peer-to-peer online money exchange. Ethereum was designed as a blockchain platform. Ripple is a platform that allows companies and individuals to send currency all over the world almost instantly.

All of these have a niche to fit, and they have a business model to go with them. This makes them a good investment to work with. If you are not able to see this business model, or the business model simply seems to make the user money or to beat Bitcoin, then it is not a good currency to work with.

Look At Some Communities About The Currency

While you are doing your research, it is a good idea to visit some cryptocurrency communities. You can look at these in general, such as ones that cover all cryptocurrencies, and ones that are specific to the currency you want to work with. These communities are full of people who know everything about cryptocurrencies, making it the perfect place to learn what you need.

The first thing that you can look at with these communities is to ask your questions. If you are unsure about using a particular currency or you have questions before you get started, then this is the place to get your questions answered. There are beginners and experts alike on these communities, so it is the perfect place to learn something new.

If you are considering a new currency, one that doesn't have a ton of research about it, then you should bring it up in these communities. Those with some technical knowledge, or even some who have been investing for a longer time, will be able to discuss it with you and help you figure out whether it is the right investment for you.

Look for Something That Seems Off

If, while you are doing your research, you feel that something is off about the currency, then it is not a good one to invest in. There are a ton of good cryptocurrencies that you can invest in, but there are also a lot of scams out there. When something seems off, it usually is – so stay away from these currencies.

You need to be careful when it comes to investing your money. Many of the currencies on the market are there to fit a need for the users. They offer a way to send money, a way to work with the blockchain, or a payment method online for example. However, there are currencies out there that were created just to make the creator rich. Running into one of the later currencies is a bad idea because it won't last long and you will end up losing money.

When you are ready to get started with investing in cryptocurrencies, the most important thing that you can concentrate on is finding a currency that will help you earn money. And with over 1000 currencies available, picking out the right one will be difficult. Looking at the characteristics above, and considering one of the four big names that we will discuss below, can make it easier to invest in a cryptocurrency that will bring in a lot of money.

Chapter 3: All About Bitcoin

- When it was developed: 2009
- The creator: Satoshi Nakamoto
- Market Cap: $193.79 billion

More About Bitcoin

The first currency we will look at is Bitcoin. This is a digital currency that can only be traded online. Anyone who has some fiat currency to exchange and an internet connection can use Bitcoin, regardless of their location. Since it is a digital currency, you will not be able to print off paper copies of it. But, you can send and receive money and even invest in this currency just like you can with fiat currency.

This currency was the first successful cryptocurrency. It was developed by Satoshi Nakamoto, who wrote white papers on how this currency should be created and used. No one knows who this individual or group is, but they came up with the idea of Bitcoin and helped to get this currency up and running.

A good benefit of Bitcoin is that it is considered decentralized. What this means is that there is no central authority, like the government of a country, controlling how the currency works. Instead, this currency relies on a complex mathematical equation to help keep it running.

When it comes to Bitcoin, you will work with blockchain technology. The blockchain is responsible for taking care of all the transactions that occur on the network. It is transparent because all users on the network can view this ledger when they would like. However, the blockchain can keep your information safe based on the work of the miners.

There are also no worries about over inflation in the market. There are only 21 million coins created with Bitcoin, and they are not released all at once. When a miner has created a secure code to protect the transaction information on the blockchain, they will be rewarded with some coins. This helps to slowly release some more coins into the network.

Users can work with Bitcoin just like they would with their fiat currency, as long as the work is done online. They can make purchases from approved retailers. They can send money to others regardless of where they are located throughout the world. They can even receive money from others. Some people have found that investing in Bitcoin has been highly profitable.

The transactions on Bitcoin are simple and fast. Rather than waiting a few days to send money to someone like you would through a bank or financial institution, you can get it done within a few minutes. In addition, the fees for sending this money through the blockchain are very small, much less than you would pay through your personal bank.

There are also a growing number of merchants who are willing to accept Bitcoin as a form of payment. The number is still small, but there are sure to be more options as time goes on. Before long, you should be able to shop at many of your favorite stores online using Bitcoin to make the payment.

Joining Bitcoin is pretty easy to do. Set up an account with Coinbase and pick out a good wallet, and you are set to go. You may have to wait a few days to link up a payment method, but after that, you can start using your coins right away.

Because Bitcoin has been so successful, there are many other cryptocurrencies available on the market now. Some of them are meant to be payment methods like Bitcoin, and others are used in different ways. Bitcoin is still considered one of the biggest cryptocurrencies around and isn't planning on going anywhere.

The Value of Bitcoin

The biggest question that many people have when they are first considering Bitcoin is how much it is worth. Just like with any type of currency you are working with, the value of Bitcoin can go up and down quite a bit from day to day. And as more people begin to learn about Bitcoin and decide that they want to join the market, the value of Bitcoin will continue to go up.

You will notice that some wide fluctuations occur in Bitcoin, even throughout the same day. The idea of digital currencies is still pretty new, and while it is available all throughout the world, there are some who are still experimenting with it to see if this kind of currency will stay around for the long-term. Overall though, the value of Bitcoin has gone up quite a bit, which has made it a good investment opportunity.

For example, the value of Bitcoin at one point in October of 2017 reached USD 6000, and by December, it was up above $18,000. Back in February of 2017, the value of a Bitcoin was only $2500. This is a huge increase in less than a year, and while there have been some major dips that have occurred during this time, they haven't really stopped the value of Bitcoin from going up.

While the value of Bitcoin has taken a little bit of a dip and is now hovering around $11,000, it still has seen a huge increase in value. Before you decide to invest or trade in Bitcoin, look up the Bitcoin exchange rate to find out exactly how much Bitcoin is worth when you are ready to get started.

These high jumps in the value of Bitcoin means that it is a great investment opportunity. As long as you learn to read the market and watch out for some potential downturns, such as what happened in January 2018 with Bitcoin, this can be a great way to invest your money and make a profit in return.

The value of Bitcoin, and many of the other digital currencies, is determined by the users and the supply of coins in the market. The more demand there is for the coins, and the lower the supply of these coins, the higher the value of the currencies.

The Top Reasons to Use Bitcoin

There are a lot of reasons that you should consider using Bitcoin when you are ready to get started with investing. Some of the top reasons to invest in Bitcoin (or even to use it for your own personal reasons) include:

- No government intervention
- One of the first currencies, making it one of the best
- Huge market cap
- Lots of demand in this market
- Low transaction fees to make it easier to send and receive money
- A growing number of retailers who accept Bitcoin as a payment method
- Easy to sign up for
- Many options to invest in this currency
- Ability to keep your personal information safe
- Fast transactions that only take a few minutes to complete, rather than a few days.
- More merchants than ever willing to take Bitcoin as a form of payment for goods and services.
- Uses the blockchain which provides security and transparency in the market.

If you are looking for a good cryptocurrency to start investing in, then Bitcoin is one of the best options for you.

Chapter 4: All About Ethereum

- When it was developed: Proposed in 2013, but was funded in 2014
- The creator: Proposed by Vitalik Buterin
- Market Cap: $109 billion

More About Ethereum

Another cryptocurrency that you can consider investing in is known as Ethereum. This one is a bit different than Bitcoin. It is not designed to be used as a traditional payment method. Instead, this currency focuses on developing the blockchain technology. While the two are different, Ethereum is quickly growing, and the market cap is only slightly below that of Bitcoin.

Before Ethereum came around, creating a new blockchain application would need a lot of work. You would need significant resources, mathematics, cryptography, and coding to make this happen. This really slowed down the progress of the blockchain because very few people were able to create these applications.

Now, things are changing. Thanks to the open source blockchain available through the Ethereum platform, many applications that would have been impossible a few years ago, or at least would have taken a few years o complete, are not around and being used faster than ever before. From regulatory compliance to electronic voting and so much more, Ethereum has allowed blockchain to come into the future.

To keep things simple, Ethereum is an open software platform that has been based on the blockchain technology. It is designed to enable developers to build and then deploy their own decentralized applications. The developer will not have to start from scratch to make these applications, which saves them a lot of time and money. And since they no longer need a lot of technical backgrounds to get started, it is easier for anyone with an idea to put it into action.

Just like with Bitcoin, Ethereum is distributed on a public blockchain network. There are a few important technical differences between Bitcoin and Ethereum, the biggest distinction is that they will differ in their purpose and in their capability.

For example, Bitcoin is one of the applications of blockchain technology. It uses the blockchain to help users to make purchases through Bitcoin payments. Bitcoin is an example of what people could create when they use the Ethereum platform. Ethereum is not used as a payment method. It is used to help run the programming code of any decentralized application that someone wants to develop.

Within the blockchain that helps o run Ethereum, the miners will work to earn Ether, the coin that is in charge of fueling the network. Beyond being a tradable coin, Ether can also be used by application developers to pay for services and transaction fees that they encounter on the Ethereum network.

One cool thing that can be done with the Ethereum network is smart contracts. Smart contracts are self-executing contracts that can help bring together two parties, without the need of a third-party knowing their business or charging large fees for the work.

These smart contracts are run by a computer code that will be used to help facilitate the exchange of anything of value, including shares, property, content, and money. When it runs on the blockchain, these smart contracts will start acting like a self-operating computer program that will execute on its own when certain conditions are met.

These contracts are really nice. They provide the benefits and the protections of a regular contract, but they do not need that third-party present to ensure they are executed properly. This can save you a lot of money and time. In addition, since these smart contracts are run on a blockchain they will run as they are programmed, without issues with fraud, downtime, censorship, or interference from a third party.

Ethereum is really unique. While all blockchains process code, most will be really limited. Ethereum helps to make a difference with this though. Rather than setting up limited operations that you can do, Ethereum has opened up the floor so that developers can create the operations that they want.

This means that developers can build up thousands of applications. If they can think about the application, it is possible with the Ethereum platform. This will help to bring the blockchain technology into the future.

There are many other ways that you can use Ethereum as well. Ethereum is there to help developers to build and deploy new decentralized applications. These applications serve a particular purpose to the users. For example, the Bitcoin application will enable users to work with an electronic cash system. And since these applications are made up of a code that uses the blockchain network to run, they will never be controlled by a central entity or individual.

In addition, any services that are currently centralized can use Ethereum to become decentralized. Think about all of the intermediary services that are used across countless industries. Whether you are voting, setting up the title on our car, getting a loan from a bank or purchasing a house, you are working with intermediary services.

Ethereum makes it possible to take all of these and change them into a decentralized system. The code will be designed to replace the need for people and the centralized control. You will still get all of the safety and benefits of using an intermediary, but you will be able to complete your work without a third party being present.

There are so many reasons that you should consider working with Ethereum as your cryptocurrency investment option. Whether you want to get into a currency that has a large market cap, you want to help develop blockchain technology some more, or you want a solid cryptocurrency that doesn't have as high of a cost to enter, then working with Ethereum is the option that you should choose.

The Benefits of Working with Ethereum

As you can see, there are many great benefits to choosing the Ethereum platform to help you make money with cryptocurrency investing. Some of the best benefits that you will find include:

- Makes blockchain application creation available to anyone who wants it.
- Provides a way for developers to receive coins and use them to pay for the fees and other costs of using the platform.
- Facilitates the use of smart contracts.
- Immutability: This means that a third party is not able to go through and make changes to any of the data.
- Tamper-proof and corruption proof: The apps that are based on this network are formed around the idea of consensus. This makes it really hard for any one person or group to censor things.
- Secure: This system does not have a central point of failure, and it is secured with the help of cryptography applications. This helps to prevent issues with fraudulent activities and hacking attacks.
- Zero downtime: The apps that are created on this network will never go down, and it is impossible to switch them off.

Ethereum is a great cryptocurrency to invest in. It has a large market cap and a ton of potential for new users to come onto the market, and yet it costs a lot less than working with Bitcoin or some of the other cryptocurrencies. This is definitely an option that you need to consider adding into your portfolio.

Chapter 5: All About Ripple

- When it was developed: 2012
- The creator: Ryan Fugger
- Market Cap: $50.19 billion

The Basics of Ripple

Ripple was released in 2012 as an iteration of Rippleplay. It is known as a real-time gross settlement system, a remittance network, and a currency exchange. Ripple uses a common ledger, one that is managed by a network of validating servers that will compare the transaction records.

Ripple is a simple system to use, and it is not going to rely on all the computer or energy-intensive proof of work like Bitcoin. Instead, this system is based on a shared public database that will use the consensus process between all the systems that are validating to ensure that integrity is maintained. The servers that do this work can belong to anyone who joins the networks, from banks to individuals.

The Ripple protocol is designed to enable direct and almost instant transfer of money between two parties, no matter where they are located. Any currency can be exchanged on this network. This means that you can transfer things like gold, any type of fiat currency, cryptocurrency, and even airline miles. You get the benefit of avoiding all the wait times and fees that come with the traditional banking system, and it is even more efficient compared to most cryptocurrency transactions.

The first question that a lot of users have is how Ripple is fundamentally different from Bitcoin. Because of the consensus mechanism and the validating servers, many users assume that Ripple is based on the blockchain technology like Bitcoin.

Yes, it does rely on all the computers agreeing to the transactions, Ripple does not rely on the blockchain. Instead, it uses what is known as a HashTree to summarize all the data into one single value. This single value will then be compared to all the validating servers.

One reason that this is a good currency to work with is that there is a lot of backing in the financial world. Banks like to use Ripple, and there are some payment providers are already coming on board to use this system, and with its ease of use and fast payment model, it is likely that more will begin to use this in the future.

Banks and other financial institutions like working with Ripple because this platform is designed for enterprise. It can be used for transferring money between two individuals, this isn't really the primary focus of this platform. Instead, Ripple was designed to move a lot of money around the world as quickly and efficiently as possible.

Since Ripple was released, it has stayed stable with a release of 35 million transactions processed without any issues. The system is set up to hold onto a lot of transactions at the same time, and it is currently able to work with 1500 transactions each second. There are also updates in place to make it up to scale to the levels that Visa handles.

This is way faster than a lot of the big cryptocurrencies that you may work with. For example, Bitcoin is only able to handle between three to six transactions per second, if you don't include the scaling layers, and Ethereum can handle about 15 transactions per second.

Unlike what is found in Litecoin, Ethereum, and Bitcoin, the Ripple token, which is known as XRP, is not mined. Instead, the coins were issued when it was released, similar to how a company will issue their stocks when it incorporates. This company picked out a number, which was 100 billion, and then issued that many coins to be used in the market.

As a type of technology, Ripple has a real value. However, the token for Ripple, XRP, seems to have a negligible use case. In fact, this token has very little use inside the network and Ripple has made plans to phase it out.

There are 100 billion of these tokens that were originally released with the Ripple company. The company promises, at least at this time, that this is all the tokens that there will ever be. This may change in the future, but it seems to be pretty successful at this rate right now.

The token is set up to be the tool that is fungible with the digital asset. Ripple can settle up a payment in less than four seconds through XRP, and then it is available and spendable. The use of this token will be completely independent of the Ripple network in general. What this means is that banks don't need to have the token to send money to other people. You can use these tokens, but it is possible to do the transactions without them as well.

So, why is there a lot of hype about working with Ripple? First, there are a lot of backers in the financial world because it is an easy and fast method of sending money, any type of money, to people all around the world.

In addition, with the rise in value of Bitcoin, there were a lot of investors who were looking for a less expensive option that would make it easier to join the cryptocurrency market while still making money. Options like Ripple were great choices because it cost only a few dollars to get into the market, rather than almost $20,000 that Bitcoin was near at one point.

With all the good things that come with Ripple, it is definitely a currency that will continue to grow. You can send and receive money no matter where you live in the world or what currency you are using. It is fast and efficient. And you don't even need to have some of the coins to use this network. For those who are expanding out their portfolio, or who want to work with a cryptocurrency that is not Bitcoin, Ripple is one of the best options to choose.

The Reasons to Invest In Ripple

Ripple is a little bit different than the other two cryptocurrencies that we talked about, but this is one of the benefits of working with it rather than one of the others. Bitcoin is a good option if you want to work with a payment system and Ethereum is a good option if you want to invest in a blockchain platform.

But Ripple is a good option for those who want to invest in a money transfer system that is taking over the financial world. Some of the benefits that you can get from working with the Ripple system includes:

- Has a good market cap
- Can help others to send and receive money, regardless of which currency they are using or where they are located in the world.
- Can use the system whether you have the Ripple coins or not
- Many big backers behind it, such as banks and other financial institutions.
- Can be used by individuals as well as big corporations to move money quickly.
- Can send money quickly.

If you are looking for a unique cryptocurrency to work with or you want to expand out your portfolio with a new currency, then Ripple provides plenty of reasons to help you do this.

Chapter 6: All About Litecoin

- When it was developed: 2011
- The creator: Charlie Lee
- Market Cap: $10.33 billion

The Basics of Litecoin

Litecoin was originally released in 2011 and is an alternative cryptocurrency that follows the same model as Bitcoin. It was developed by Charlie Lee, an MIT graduate, and a former Google engineer. Litecoin is based on an open source global payment network that doesn't have a central authority controlling it.

This currency will be similar to Bitcoin, but it differs in some key points such as a faster block generation rate, and it will use scrypt as a proof of work scheme rather than the blockchain.

When Litecoin was launched, it had the aim of being the silver to Bitcoin's gold. Since the time that Litecoin came out, it has gained a lot of popularity, although it has one of the lowest market caps of any currency on our list.

There are a lot of things to like about Litecoin. This currency is a peer-to-peer internet currency. It is fully decentralized so you won't have to worry about a government agency or someone else taking control of this currency. It is known as a global payment network so you can use it similar to Bitcoin.

When you look at using Litecoin, you will notice that it can improve on some of the shortcomings that are found in Bitcoin. Because of this, it has earned a lot of support in the industry, and you can find a lot of liquidity and high trade volume in this currency.

May people get Litecoin and Bitcoin confused because they both work in similar ways. They have the same idea behind running them, they are used as a payment method, and so much more. Let's take a look at some of the differences between Litecoin and Bitcoin to help you see why they are so different from each other and why Litecoin may be the better cryptocurrency to go with.

	Bitcoin	Litecoin
Introduced	2009	2011
Who created	Satoshi Nakamoto	Charles Lee
How many coins	21 million	84 million
Time to generate blocks	10 minutes	2.5 minutes
Algorithm	SHA-256 (blockchain)	Scrypt
Block reward (as of June 2014)	25 BTC	50 BTC
Rewards	Halved every 210,000 block	Halved every 840,000 blocks

As a traditional user of these currencies, you may not see much of a difference between the two. You will be able to use both of them in the same manner to complete purchases and send and receive money throughout the world. There are not as many big companies that accept Litecoin right now, but the number is starting to grow.

This is a great cryptocurrency for you to work with. First, it has improved on a lot of the issues that have come up with Bitcoin throughout the year. While a typical transaction on Bitcoin will take about ten minutes to show up and process on the blockchain, this can be done in under three minutes with Litecoin. While both speeds are much faster than you can find with your traditional bank, Litecoin is by far the fastest of the two.

In addition, Litecoin has created more coins to be released. Many critics of Bitcoin are worried about how quickly those coins will be gone. There are only 21 million on the Bitcoin network, and people worry that as the market keeps growing the way that it does, these coins will not be enough.

With the Litecoin network, there are 84 million coins. This allows the currency to continue to grow in ways that are not possible with some of the other currencies.

The amount of coins that are rewarded for mining on the Litecoin network is larger. You can earn twice as many coins for the work through Litecoin than you can do with Bitcoin. While the value of Litecoin is a lot less right now, which means that the coins are worth less than the Bitcoin if Litecoin starts to take off and increase in value, the reward will be much higher in the future.

As an investor, this is a good currency to work in. It is much cheaper to get started in Litecoin. You can purchase more of the coins for a lower cost than you were able to do with Bitcoin right now. And with all the benefits and features that come with Litecoin, it is likely that this currency will keep on growing and the value of those coins will increase.

The Benefits of Using Litecoin

If you are looking to become an investor in a currency that is very similar to Bitcoin, but costs a lot less and has some improvements over Bitcoin, then Litecoin is the right option for you. Some of the benefits of investing in Litecoin include:

- It improves upon the Bitcoin network while still being a payment method.
- Has more coins available to use
- It offers a bigger profit to those who are mining
- It can process transactions in less than two minutes.
- The cost of joining the network is much lower than with other currencies
- Relies on a consensus system, but not on the blockchain.

Working with Litecoin can be a great option for a new investor. Often Bitcoin will be too expensive to get started in for new investors. But with the help of Litecoin, you can work with a currency that is faster and more efficient, although used in the same manner, while not having to come up with as much initial investment.

Chapter 7: The Future of These Cryptocurrencies

The idea of cryptocurrency is relatively new. It wasn't until 2009 when Bitcoin was released on the world when a successful, decentralized currency was released. There were several other attempts at doing this, but they focused too much on third-party interference that they didn't stand a chance. Ever since Bitcoin was released, the news about cryptocurrency has grown like crazy, and there are now many other cryptocurrencies that are found on the market.

With all the popularity of Bitcoin and the other cryptocurrencies, there is some question about how they will do in the future. These currencies are so new, and they have nothing on the market that is similar. This makes it hard to figure out how well these currencies will do in the future. And with the high volatility that comes with these currencies, many people wonder if they will fade out soon or are here to stay.

Increased Scrutiny

One thing that you will find with some of these digital currencies is that there will be an increased scrutiny around them. The anonymity on the network and the decentralization can be great benefits for most users, but it has also made these currencies favorable to illegal activities. In fact, the beginning of many of these coins is riddled with issues of weapons procurement, smuggling, drug peddling, and even money laundering.

Because of these illegal activities, there has been a lot of attention brought to these currencies, and it is not in the best light. Many powerful regulatory agencies are working against these cryptocurrencies, placing rules in effect that limit what can be done on these currencies.

While it is understandable that these agencies want to stop illegal activities, the more these agencies get involved in the world of cryptocurrency and how it runs, the harder it will be to attract new users. One of the benefits of using cryptocurrencies is that you don't have to worry about government regulation and if a government is getting involved, it takes away the trust from the cryptocurrency.

Despite the fact that these cryptocurrencies are decentralized, it seems that some governments and other agencies want to get involved. Depending on how much scrutiny is given to the currencies, and how much involvement from the government agencies, it could negatively affect these currencies in the future.

Less Competition

Over time, it is likely that there will be less competition within the cryptocurrency market. These currencies are so popular right now that it seems everyone is jumping on board. Some are legitimate currencies that want to fill a niche or a need, but many are created to make money for the creator.

The ones that are solid and there to fill a need will stay around for the long-term. All the others are likely to fail. This allows for less competition in the market. If you chose one of the cryptocurrencies that doesn't do well in the market, this might not be the best news. But for most investors, this will mean bigger profits from the ones that are left behind.

Government Interference

The biggest thing that will determine how cryptocurrencies will do in the future is government interference. Each government will react to cryptocurrencies differently, and this will determine what changes, if any, that will happen with these currencies.

Let's look at an example of how this works. There is increasing pressure from the IRS to enforce regulations on cryptocurrencies. The idea here is that people who go on these digital currency markets can remain anonymous and may be doing illegal activities like money laundering.

The IRS and other government agencies want to require exchange sites to collect personal information about users before they can join a new network or exchange any money. The idea here is that the IRS would be able to collect information about those who are using the network and make sure that no one is hiding money on one of these networks.

While this may sound like a good intentioned idea, it does run into some problems. It takes away some of the anonymity that users of cryptocurrencies have come to expect. This alone may be able to turn a few users away from these networks for good.

This is just one example of what could happen with government interference. There are different reactions from each country. China has restricted use to these currencies because it developed its own blockchain with its borders. Switzerland and other places in Europe are jumping on board because they see the benefit of facilitating trade and more across borders thanks to these currencies. As you can imagine, the way that a country reacts to these currencies will greatly influence how that currency survives in that area.

The Future

There are a few limitations that cryptocurrencies are facing. Some of them, such as your coins being erased by a hacker or a computer crash, will be pretty easy for technological advances to fix. What is harder is some of the other issues, such as more regulations and government scrutiny, will be harder for the cryptocurrency market to get over.

While there are more and more users and merchants who are accepting these currencies, there is still a long way to go. To help these currencies to grow and stay around, there needs to be more acceptance by the consumer. When consumers start to accept these currencies, it is more likely for the merchants to accept them as payments as well.

In addition, if a cryptocurrency would like to become part of the regular financial system, there are a lot of divergent criteria that it needs to meet. It needs to be complex mathematically to avoid hacker attacks, but still be easy enough for consumers to understand. They need to be decentralized while still having enough safeguards that the average consumer is comfortable using them. And they need to be able to provide consumers with some anonymity to protect their privacy while avoiding illegal activities.

As you can see, there is a lot that these cryptocurrencies need to be able to do to survive in the future. There are several that are already set up to handle some of these challenges, or who are already making the necessary changes. The ones that are not able to keep up with all of this will likely not make it into the future.

Is It A Safe Investment?

The big question now is whether investing in cryptocurrency is worth it. There are already a lot of risks in investing with this market and the fact that it may not be around to stay, especially with all the outside forces going against it, make the risk even higher.

If you are considering investing in cryptocurrencies, you need to remember that you are working with a true investment. Treat it just like you would other highly speculative ventures. There is a risk in this market, and since there isn't an intrinsic value with the currency, you need to be really careful.

Investing in cryptocurrency can be a great way for you to earn some money, especially if you can pick out a good currency to invest in. But you need to be aware of the risks that come with this investment and how they will affect how much you will earn before entering the market.

Part 3: Getting Started with Cryptocurrency

Chapter 1: Setting Up Your Cryptocurrency Wallet

Before you can get started with investing in cryptocurrency, you need to make sure that you have a place to store the coins you are using. Sine, you are not able to print off the coins and carry them around with you, and you are not able to leave these currencies in a bank, you need to find someplace else to store these coins. This is where a cryptocurrency wallet can come into play.

Cryptocurrency wallets are software programs that make it easy to store the private and the public keys of your coins. You can use these keys to interact with the blockchain to monitor your balance, send and receive money, and conduct other operations. When someone sends you some new coins, they are essentially signing off their ownership of the coins and giving them to the address assigned to your wallet. To use these coins, the private key that is stored in your wallet needs to match the public address the currency is being assigned to.

When these two keys match up, the balance that is inside your digital wallet will increase, while the amount in the sender's wallet will decrease. Remember that with this process, there isn't an actual exchange of coins like there is with traditional currencies. The transaction will show up on the blockchain though, and you will see a change in the balance of your wallet.

The types of wallets

The first thing that you need to decide is which kind of wallet that you want to use. There are a number of factors that you can consider when it comes to choosing a wallet including:

- What features you want to see
- How often you will use the coins
- How secure do you want to have your wallet
- How readily available you want the coins to be

There are a few types of wallets that you can use when you are ready to store your coins. Some of these will provide better access to the coins, but the security may be lacking in some places. Others may take a few more steps before you can use the coins, but they can make your coins more secure to use.

The main types of wallets that you can choose to store your cryptocurrency includes:

Online

Online wallets will usually run in the cloud. These are nice to use because you can access them from any device that you would like and it doesn't matter your current location. They are also convenient because you don't have to take any extra steps before you can start using the coins.

There are a lot of online wallets to choose from. You can keep things easy and simply use the wallet that your exchange site provides to you. You can also choose from other wallets based on their security, their features and more.

The biggest issue with these online wallets is that they are more susceptible to hackers because all the information is online. If a hacker gets onto the network or you get a virus, it can be hard to keep those coins secure, and you may lose them.

For those who are looking to invest their coins, this is not the best option. Leaving them around in an online wallet can make it easier for hackers to get ahold of them. However, if you are looking to use the coins right away after you exchange them, then this option is very convenient to use.

Hardware wallet

Another option that you can choose is the hardware, also called desktop wallet. Like this one sounds, you would download the wallet and install it on the desktop of your laptop or PC. These are not as accessible as the online wallets because you have to use your own personal computer to get the coins. But since the coins are still on your computer, it is still pretty easy to use them whenever you would like.

The good news is that these add on an extra level of protection. If someone wanted to get ahold of the coins in a desktop wallet, they would need to gain access to your computer. You will need to make sure that you have the latest operating system and antivirus on your computer to ensure that no one can get your coins.

This is a good option to use for many investors. It is much safer for the coins compared to the online wallet, but you will still be able to use the coins if you need to.

Cold storage or paper wallet

If you really want to get a high level of security, then you need to rely on cold storage. This option requires you to print off your private and public keys and then store them somewhere that is on your computer. Someone would have to get ahold of the piece of paper before they can steal your coins. It is a bit harder to get the cons back online and use them, but for long-term investors who want to keep the coins safe, this is the best option.

Are These Wallets Secure?

We talked about the security of these wallets a bit above, and each one will be able to provide you with a degree of security. Keeping the coins in an online wallet is riskier than leaving them in cold storage, but you need to pick the one that is right for you.

If you are considering using an online wallet because of the convenience, but you are worried about how safe and secure your coins will be, there are a few precautions that you can take. These precautions include:

Backup the wallet: keep a bit of your currency in the wallet to use as you would like, but then place the majority of the funds in a more secure wallet. This way, if someone gets ahold of your wallet, you only stand to lose a little bit of the money. The rest can be proven as yours based on your chosen wallet method.
Update your software: When using an online wallet, it is a good idea to keep all of your software up to date. This makes it harder for a hacker to get in.

Add some extra security: The more security that you can provide, the better. Pick out complex and long passwords and make sure that this password is required before funds can be released. Use a wallet that has a good reputation, and go with ones that have extra security layers. Some things to look for include pin requirements and two-factor authentication.

How Do I Pick Out A Wallet?

While we have spent some time talking about the various wallets that you can use, you may still be wondering which wallet is the right one for you. There are a few questions that you can ask yourself to help come up with the right wallet for all your cryptocurrency needs. Some of the questions that you should ask include:

- Are you looking to use your wallet for everyday purchases, or do you plan to invest your money and use the buy and hold strategy?
- Are you going to work with one currency or several currencies?
- Do you need to be able to get ahold of your wallet from anywhere, or is it fine to only access it when at home?

Answering these questions will make it so much easier to determine which type of wallet is the right one for you.

Chapter 2: The Definitions You Need to Work in Cryptocurrency

When it comes to working with cryptocurrency, there will be many different terms that you will come across. These terms are new since these currencies are new, but it is still important to learn what they all mean. This will make it easier for you to join the network and complete your investments. Some of the common terms that you should learn include:

Altcoin: Any cryptocurrency that is not Bitcoin. These currencies account for fifty percent of the market capitalization for cryptocurrency.

Consensus: A project community coming to agreement on proposed changes to the project's network protocol.

Decentralization: This is a network where no group or person is in control. With cryptocurrency, it means that no one authority or government is controlling how the currency works.

Dump: When the value of a particular cryptocurrency decreases quickly. This will occur when many of the main holders of the currency sell off their coins.

FUD: This is an acronym for fear, uncertainty, and doubt. It is often going to refer to false news that is sent out to attack either one coin in specific or to attack the market of cryptocurrency in general.

Hard fork: This is when there is a change in the underlying consensus rules of a cryptocurrency and for which you are not able to make it compatible with older versions.

Pre-mine or Instamine: This is the allocation of coins in a cryptocurrency before the project is launched (pre-mine) or the coins that are allocated quickly when the project is first started (instamine).

Pump: When the value of the cryptocurrency increases really fast, based on self-promotion of that particular cryptocurrency.

Scam: A cryptocurrency that is around simply because the creator wanted to make money for themselves.

Shill: a person who has the job of relentlessly promoting a specific cryptocurrency. The point here is to get the news out about that particular cryptocurrency in the hopes that the currency will start to gain value.

Working in cryptocurrencies can be a great way to send and receive payments while also using the currency as a form of investing. Use the terms above to help you enter into the market and to ensure that you can get the best results possible. They will help you to figure out when a currency is the right one to go with and when one may not be worth your time.

Chapter 3: Day Trading vs. Buy and Hold

When it comes to investing in cryptocurrency, there are many different methods that you can work with. You can invest your money into the blockchain technology, you can choose to invest in the Bitcoin company on the stock market, and so much more. But the two most popular trading strategies that you can go with include day trading and the buy and hold strategy.

Both of these strategies can be really effective in helping you to make money and see results in the cryptocurrency market. It is all about whether you would like to work with a long-term strategy or a short-term strategy. It also depends on how much time you would like to spend doing the investment.

The Basics Of Day Trading

Day trading is a strategy where you will purchase into a cryptocurrency and then sell the coins on the same day. While the majority of these currencies are increasing in value, there are a lot of ups and downs in the market throughout the day. These movements are not all that big, but they can help you make a good profit.

You will basically do a lot of little trades through the week and then earn a lot of profit. Each individual trade is not going to bring in a ton of profit, but it can add up to many trades.

You will need to spend some time on this strategy to make money though. You need to look at the market and know the market value of each currency you want to trade in. When the coin goes below this market value, you will make a purchase. Then, when the coin goes to or above market value, you will exchange it out and make a profit.

The benefits of day trading

There are many benefits to using the day trading strategy. Some of these benefits include:

- Earn money each day
- Take advantage of temporary ups and downs in the market
- Easy to understand
- Can earn a profit even in a down market
- Has the potential for a lot of profit

The negatives of day trading

For some people, the day trading strategy is one of the best ones to choose. You can make a lot of money and really learn a lot about the cryptocurrency market. But the day trading strategy is not the right one for everyone. Some of the negatives of going with this strategy include:

- Takes a lot of research
- Will take a lot of time looking at the market
- The market can easily go against your trade
- Stressful
- The costs can outweigh the profits if you are not careful

The Basics Of The Buy And Hold Strategy

As a beginner, you may find that working with the buy and hold strategy is more your speed. This option is a long-term investment strategy, which means that you will need to wait a bit to earn your money back. However, there really isn't as much work with this option, and you have the potential to earn a lot of money if the value of your chosen currency takes off.

The benefits of the buy and hold strategy

This is really a simple strategy to work with. You will enter the market, leave your coins in a safe wallet, and then let it grow. When you are ready, you will take the money out and keep the profit. Some of the benefits of this currency include:

- Easy to work with

- Very little that you need to do once the money is in the account.
- Can take the money out whenever you would like.
- Only need to watch the market on occasion

The negatives of the buy and hold strategy

While this is the preferred trading strategy for beginners, there are some negatives to working with the buy and hold strategy. Some of the negatives of this strategy include:

You can't make money each day and have to wait for your profit. The market can turn quickly, and you could lose all your profits if you don't watch the market.

Which Strategy Is The Best?

If you are trying to decide which strategy to work with, it is best to go with the buy and hold strategy. Some investors like to work with the day trading strategy, but this requires a lot of work and is pretty risky compared to how much profit you can earn.

On the other hand, working with the buy and hold strategy is relatively simple. You need to add some money to the market and then leave it in a safe and secure wallet of your choice. Then, you need to watch the market and watch your money grow. If you picked out a good currency, the value will increase over time.

Outside of watching the market and making sure that no signs are pointing to a reversal of the market. Then, either after a certain amount of time, a certain amount of profit, or you see a downturn in the market, you will exchange your coins back out for your fiat currency and take home the profit.

That is really all there is to it. A good example of this is with Bitcoin. Back in February of 2017, the value of Bitcoin stood around $2500 a coin. As time went on, the value went way up, reaching almost $20,000 a coin in December 2017. If you had purchased back in

February and let your coins sit in the wallet until December, you could have earned a huge profit without having to do any work.

For a beginner investor, this is one of the best options that you can go with. You just need to come up with some upfront money and a good secure wallet, and you are set.

Both of these trading strategies can help you to make some good money in cryptocurrency. They allow you to work with this growing market to earn a profit. However, if you are new to investing and want to put in as little work as possible while earning a good profit, then it is a good idea to work with the buy and hold strategy.

Chapter 4: What is the Buy and Hold Strategy

The buy and hold strategy is one of the best strategies to use in cryptocurrency. This strategy is not going to take much research or time, but it has the best potential to help you earn a ton of money in this market. As long as you purchase the currency at a low point and the market keeps going up in value, you stand to make some money.

Getting started with the buy and hold strategy is simple. Sign up for your own account on the chosen cryptocurrency network and sign up for an exchange site, if you have not done this already. When you are ready, you simply need to exchange some of your fiat money out for the cryptocurrency and place it in a secure wallet.

From here, you just need to wait. You must make sure that you pick a secure wallet though. Hackers love to get ahold of coins, and it is likely that you will leave your coins in the wallet for at least a few months, if not for a much longer time. Choosing a hardware wallet or cold storage will make it easier to keep your coins safe.

With this strategy, you are waiting for the value of the cryptocurrency to go up. Sometimes this can happen within a few months, and other times it may require you to wait a few years before you see any significant profits. You need to have patience with this kind of strategy, but as long as you pick a good cryptocurrency and watch the market, you are sure to see profits with this strategy.

During this time, you must watch the market though. There are often indicators that will let you know when it is time to purchase the currency and when it is time to sell. If you stay in the market too long, you may end up losing your profits when the currency goes down again.

While the market for many cryptocurrencies is generally going up, there are times when the currency will go down or level out and stop growing. Watching the market and looking through charts can help you see these signs when deciding whether to use the currency for your investment. Or, if you are already in the market, you can use these charts to determine if it is time to leave the market.

Let's take a look at an example of this. In December of 2017, the value of Bitcoin went up to more than $18,000 a coin. Then in January, the price of the coins started to go down, and by the end of the month, the value of this currency was $11,000.

If you had joined the market a few months before December, there are a few things that could have happened. You may have been watching the market, and when it got to $18,000, you may have seen that it indicated that the market was about to go down. Seeing these, you would exchange your coins out for your fiat currency and take a handsome profit.

However, some newer investors may have assumed that the currency would continue to climb more and more. They wouldn't have spent time looking at the charts and figures, and in the process, they would have missed out on the indicators telling them that the market was about to go down. If they waited a few weeks longer, their profits would be gone as the market went down. Depending on the price when they purchased the currency, they may have even lost money in this transaction.

Now, most currencies are not going to have the large value that Bitcoin does, but it does provide an example of what can happen in the market if you are not paying attention.

The buy and hold strategy can work well with many newer currencies. It is likely that there won't be any huge bumps in Bitcoin in the near future. This currency is getting near its leveling out point, and the cost of entry is pretty high at more than $11,000 per coin.

However, there are a lot of other currencies, such as Litecoin, Ethereum, and more, that are just as solid without costing as much right now. You could join Ethereum for about $368 per coin.

Since these coins are less expensive to join in, you can purchase more. And if you are willing to hold onto the currency for a few years, you can turn these coins into some good money. Let's say that you purchased ten Ethereum coins. Then in two years, the value of Ethereum is $1000 per coin.

This means that you purchased ten coins for $3,680 today, but within two years, the value of your coins would be $10,000. You make a profit of more than $6000, just for keeping your money in the exchange for a few years. The more that the value of Ethereum, or any currency, goes up, the more profit you can bring home.

The buy and hold strategy is one of the best cryptocurrency strategies for you to use. It is simple and only requires you to put some money into the network and then hold onto it for some time. You must pick out a secure wallet and a good performing currency, but you don't need to watch the market non-stop, and it doesn't require you to spend all day doing work. As a beginner who wants to learn more about this market, who wants to earn money, but who doesn't want to have a lot of work in the process.

Chapter 5: What is the Day Trading Strategy

Some people decide that they do not want to wait around to earn their profits through the buy and hold strategy. While that one may seem easier, they are worried that the market will crash soon and they don't' want to have coins in the market and lose them all. With day trading, you can earn money even in a bad market. You will purchase the coins sometime during the day, and then you must sell them during the same day.

Day trading allows you to earn little profits during the day. It takes advantage of the little ups and downs that occur during the market and depending on how the market is doing, you may be able to do several trades during the same day. The amount that you make on each trade is not going to be much, but it adds up pretty quickly.

Day trading will require a lot of research and charts to be successful. You will realize that while the overall market of the cryptocurrency is going upwards, there are variations of up and down at different times of the day. You want to pay attention to these ups and downs because they will help you to earn your money with this strategy.

While you are looking at these charts, you want to look at the market value. This is the median line between the highs and lows of that particular day. This line is important because it tells you the average that people are willing to pay for the coins.

From here, you will better be able to determine when to purchase the coins. When the value of the coins falls below the market value, you will make a purchase. Then, when the value of the coins goes up to market value or higher, you will sell the coins to make a purchase. The lower below market value the coins can fall, the more profit you will be able to make.

When you purchase below market value, you can increase your chances of earning a profit. Your coins only need to go up a little bit in value for you to make a profit. Remember that you are not going to earn a huge profit with each trade, but earning a little bit will add up over all your trades.

The length of your trades will never last more than one day. Depending on the market, you may have to wait all day between making a purchase and selling the coins. On other days, you may do the whole trade within one hour or less.

As long as you sell the coins before the end of the day, it is fine to sell them at any time during that day. If it only takes an hour to complete a trade, get back to your charts and do another trade or two during that same day.

There are a few things that you need to consider before you decide to go with day trading. The first thing is that you must be able to complete all trades on the same day. Since these markets are open 24/7 all around the world, it is easy to consider leaving your coins on the market overnight and waiting to see what will happen.

This is a bad idea for your investment. Things can happen in the market due to factors in other countries, and you have no control over them. If you are awake when these happen, you can get out of the market and limit your losses. But if you are asleep, your losses can just keep happening.

It is always best to take the currency out of the market before you go to bed, even if you are losing money. You can start fresh in the morning. But keeping your money in the market when you are not able to watch it can often lead to disaster.

Another issue to consider is the fees that your exchange site is charging. Each time that you exchange your fiat currency for a cryptocurrency, and then you exchange it back, the site you use will charge you a small fee. This fee is not a big deal in most cases. But when you do a lot of exchanges, such as what happens with day trading, it can certainly add up.

Day trading is a great way to earn money in the cryptocurrency market. It takes advantage of the ups and downs that occur naturally in the market. It does take some time and effort and will require you to make decisions quickly. But for those who are looking for an exciting way to earn money in this market, day trading may be the option for you.

Chapter 6: Top Cryptocurrency Analysts and Investors to Follow as a Beginner

When you are ready to get started with investing in cryptocurrency, it is best to follow some of those who have already seen success in the industry. Following the right analysts and some of those who have made money in the industry already can help you to see when things will change in a currency, to figure out which currency to follow, and even to pick out which strategy that you would like to work with. Here are some of the top analysts and investors that you should follow when you are ready to work with cryptocurrency investing.

The Best Analysts

Chris Burniske
@cburniske
32,000 followers

Chris is one of the best analysts on the market. He started out his career with Wall Street, which helped him to prepare for analyzing the world of cryptocurrencies. His paper about cryptocurrencies, "Ringing the Bell on a New Asset Class" is a top book on Amazon. If you will follow one person to help with your investment, then this is the guy. His analysis are behind many millionaires in the cryptocurrency market.

Willy Woo
@woonomic
31,000 followers

Willy has made some of the most creative charts in this market. While most of the experience that he has in this market is independent, his insights have been shared all across the internet including on his personal website, Twitter, and even CoinDesk.

Tuur Demeester
@TuurDemeester
58,000 Followers

According to the State of Blockchain Q2 sentiment survey, Tuur is one of the top analysts in the industry. He is considered a pioneer in the industry, with his professional work going back to the very beginning of Bitcoin. Not only do his analysis take a look at the technology behind these currencies, but also the economic forces that will control them as well.

Alex Sunnarborg
@alexsunnarborg
4000 followers

Alex started out in what is known as institutional investment, but when he saw how Bitcoin was taking off, he launched Lawnmower, a platform that is meant to help make cryptocurrency investing easier than ever. After winning at Money 20/20 hackathon, Alex started to work with Coinbase and even joined Coindesk. Since that time, he has started to work with the State of the Blockchain and has shared many of his creative charts on Twitter.

Top Investors

Bob Voulgaris
@haralabob
119,000 followers

While Bob has a name that many people may not recognize, mainly because he spends more time betting on NBA games rather than on cryptocurrency investing, he has become a successful investor in these currencies. He has traded in cryptocurrencies since the very beginning and has even gotten a few other big names to join the market.

Peter Brandt
@PeterLBrandt
72,000 followers

Peter has had a successful career in trading for many years but now devotes his time to being a Bitcoin trader. Many other traders have been able to learn from him, and he has taken the time to share his skills and thoughts about cryptocurrency with others.

Tone Vays
@ToneVays
42,000 followers

Tone has a background in Wall Street that has helped him do well in the new cryptocurrency market. He is known for giving insight into some of the various politics that surround Bitcoin, and through his own chart sharing, he has been able to share a lot of trading advice.

CryptoCobain
@CryptoCobain
55,000 followers

This is a pseudonym that is used to help protect the identity of this trader, and it is meant to be the alter ego of Kurt Coban. Despite some daily commentary and the idea that he had to quit from the band, CryptoCobain helps to share a lot of helpful insights to those who want to join this network. You will be able to learn about which coins may be about to take a pump, portfolio allocation, and even risk management.

Consider following some of these individuals to learn a lot more about the cryptocurrency network and how to get started, while making more money in the process.

Chapter 7: What Makes a Coin a Good Investment?

When it is time to invest in a cryptocurrency, you want to make sure that you are picking one that will bring you a good amount of money. There are more than 1000 cryptocurrencies on the market, but not all of them will provide you with the profit you are looking for. Here are a few of the characteristics that you should look for when you want to start investing in a safe, and profitable, cryptocurrency.

Review The History Of The Currency

A good place to start is to look at how the currency was created. Was it designed as a copy of Bitcoin? Were there some early investors who were given privileges of using the cryptocurrency ahead of everyone else? What are some of the terms that were used when the currency first began?

Remember that it is common for many altcoins to pre-mine the currency to help get the coins out there and ready to use. These coins are divided up among the early investors as well as the creators ahead of the official rules that others need to follow. You should take a look at how many of these tokens were pre-mined and what percentage of the tokens are already out in the public as well.

Knowing this information can help you out a lot. It will first tell you how many investors looked into this currency and saw it as a good one to invest in early one. The more investors who are interested in the currency, the better investment it can be. And when you take a look at the tokens, you will be able to tell the liquidity of the currency, or how easy it is to purchase and sell the currency when needed.

Who Runs The Currency?

If you can figure out who runs the currency, then the viability of this currency is not that great for the long term. When people can figure out who the leader is, it is easier for these leaders to become targets for law enforcement or for others to try and coerce them, bringing the security of the currency into question.

Is This Decentralized?

If you can figure out who runs the currency, it is likely that the currency is still centralized and you are working with an option like PayPal instead of a true cryptocurrency. When it comes to investing in a cryptocurrency, you will want to work with an option that is considered decentralized. This is appealing to many users and investors and can keep the value of your investment higher than ever.

What Is The Mission Statement?

This can be difficult to find sometimes. But if you are looking at the currency and it seems intent on fixing or replacing Bitcoin, it is best to stay away from that currency. Bitcoin is a formidable foe in the cryptocurrency market, and it has the most developers who are working on improving it and bringing it to the future. Trusting your wealth to a company that is trying to take on all these big name developers can be a big mistake.

Check The Marketing Potential

Often, the reason that a cryptocurrency becomes valuable is that a lot of people hear about it. For example, Bitcoin has become one of the biggest cryptocurrencies because it has been around a long time and it has had a lot of chance to market to people throughout the world. Add in that this currency reached over $18000 at one point, there was also a lot of news coverage that helped to keep the value high.

Many cryptocurrencies are trying to get the same kind of coverage. The more value that these currencies can gain, the better they are for your investment. So, to figure out whether a currency is a good one to invest in, it is important to analyze the marketing potential. Some questions that you can ask to check on this marketing potential includes:

- Are there any gurus or big names that are promoting the currency online?
- How professional is the website that is promoting this currency?
- Is it just a lot of regular people promoting the currency or do intelligent and important people support it?
- Is there some talk around the currency about it becoming a mainstream payment?
- What is the angle for marketing and why should others decide to invest in it?

To keep things simple, you should ask how easy it will be to convince uninformed people to buy into and start using the cryptocurrency. If your answer is that it should be easy to get others to purchase into the currency, then it is probably a good investment for you to choose.

Choosing a good cryptocurrency to invest in can take some time and effort to complete. There are a lot of options on the market, but only a few of them will actually bring you a decent profit. Make sure to take a look at some of the characteristics that we talked about above, and you are more likely to pick the right currency that will provide you with a good return on investment in no time.

Chapter 8: Tips to Help Your Trading Strategy

As a beginner in cryptocurrency investing, you are sure to have a lot of questions about how to get started. You want to make sure that you are reducing your risks and setting yourself up to earn as much money as possible. This chapter will take a look at some of the best things that you can do to make your trading strategy, no matter what it is, as successful as possible.

Pick Out a Good Strategy

Before you get into the market, consider picking out a good strategy to use. We discussed how the buy and hold strategy and the day trading strategy both work. These are great strategies to work with, but they each require different steps for you to use them successfully.

Knowing your strategy from the beginning, and sticking with it, can make it easier to see results. These strategies can help you to enter the market at the right time, and even tells you when to exit the market. Learn your strategy well and stick with it to get a profit each time.

Build Up Your Portfolio

When you first get started with investing in cryptocurrency, you may only have enough capital to work with one currency at a time. This is fine as a beginner, but as you start to earn more profits, it is a good idea to diversify your portfolio.

When you diversify your portfolio, you learn how to reduce your risks. Even if one of the currencies starts to go down, your money is spread out among other investments. You will not lose out on all your money when you diversify. You can choose to invest in several different currencies or even expand out to other investment options.

Come Up With an Enter and Exit Strategy

As an investor, it is a good idea to come up with an enter and exit strategy. The enter strategy is when you will decide to enter the market. If you go with the buy and hold strategy, you can enter at any time, although you may want to wait until the market is at a lower point.

With the day trading strategy, this becomes a bit more work. You will need to look through charts and the history of the currency to figure out what the market value of the coins are. When the coins get below this market value, you will enter the market because you are getting the coins at a deal.

You also need to have an exit strategy. This allows you to get out of the market and protect your investment. You should have an exit strategy for leaving the market when you are losing money and for when you earn money.

With the first exit point, consider how much you are comfortable with losing if the market goes down. This is where you should place that stop point. If the market goes down to this point, you withdraw from the market and cut your losses. You can always join the market later.

With the second exit point, you will pick the point where you are happy with the profit. With day trading, for example, you may decide to get out of the market once your coins reach market value again. This helps you to earn a profit and limits your risk of the market going down.

Avoid the Emotions

The whole point of having a strategy and coming up with your enter and exit strategy is to make sure the emotions stay out of the game. If you allow the emotions to come out, you will start making poor decisions that negatively affect your investments.

Many beginners have lost more money than necessary in the market because the emotions started up. They may have seen that they were losing money in the market. Instead of listening to their exit strategy, they stayed in the market in the hopes of gaining all that money back.

Unfortunately, when you become desperate for regaining your money, you stop making informed decisions. You jump on any opportunity that looks like it will earn the money back, and usually, you end up being wrong. If the emotions come around, you are in trouble.

For those who are likely to give into their emotions, investing in cryptocurrency is not the best option. These markets go up and down often, and it can be emotional and stressful. Setting up your plan ahead of time and sticking to a good strategy can help you to manage this.

Work with a Broker

As a beginner, you may want to consider working with a broker to help you make money. These cryptocurrency markets can be difficult to understand, and learning it all on your own, especially if you have never invested at all, can be very difficult. Having someone on your side can make it easier to get the work done without losing money in the process.

There are several different types of investors that you can work with. If you want to use the tools that a broker has available, but do the work on your own, that is possible. Or, if you are new and want a broker that can walk you through the process, this is possible as well. Keep in mind that each type of broker will charge different fees so look at how they get paid, and how much before you get started.

When picking out a broker, make sure to check whether they have worked in cryptocurrencies before. Some brokers will work in the stock market and in cryptocurrencies, and some will specialize only in cryptocurrency. Just check that they have experience in cryptocurrencies, so you get personalized help.

Getting into the cryptocurrency market can be a great way to make money, especially with how popular these currencies are right now. Following the tips above can make it easier than ever to make money with this investment.

Chapter 9: The Best Coins to Invest in Today

Picking out a good cryptocurrency to invest in can sometimes be a challenge. You could choose to go with some of the big names, such as Bitcoin or Ethereum. These are good options to go with if you want an easy way to get started. However, since these options are so well-known already, it is sometimes a risk to get in with them. You have to worry about whether they will keep increasing in value and there is the issue with their cost of entry being high already.

Whether you want to go with something different when you start investing, or you are looking for a way to expand out your portfolio, there are a lot of different currencies that you can choose from. Some of the best currencies to consider for investing include:

Dash

DASH is used to make instant and private payments, either in store or online, thanks to the open source platform that is hosted by all the users around the world. These payments are done instantly, so you no longer need to wait around and hope that the payment is processed through.

They are also private, which means that you will be able to protect your financial information any time that you are online. Thanks to the PrivaeSend technology used on DASH, your history and balances on the site will always remain private. And of course, DASH is secure to use. Transactions will be confirmed by more than 4500 servers around the world and a special 200 TerraHash of Xx11 ASIC computing power.

DASH provides all the safety and security that you are looking for when it comes to using a digital currency. This currency is easy to work with and will provide you with all the safety and security that you need to get things done. It has a benefit over Bitcoin in that it can be used at physical stores, and not just online stores. All of these benefits come together to help make this a great investment opportunity to work with.

Zcash

ZCash is another cryptocurrency that you can choose to work with when it is time to invest. This currency offers total confidentiality when making payments, while still being able to maintain a decentralized network with the help of the blockchain.

Unlike what you will see with Bitcoin, ZCash transactions will hide the information about the recipient, sender, and the value automatically on the blockchain. You have to hold onto the right key, which only the sender and the recipient should have, to see the contents of these transactions.

In our modern world, there are a lot of issues about confidentiality online can be a big problem. People are tired of having to worry about whether their personal information is safe when they shop or do other things online. This can even be an issue when they are using other cryptocurrencies like Bitcoin. With ZCash making it easier to keep information online private, there is sure to be a lot of interest in it in the future.

Gridcoin

If you are looking for a currency that will help out charities, especially those that are into scientific research, then Gridcoin is the option for you. Gridcoin provides benefits to humanity because it provides contributions to scientific research. It is also the only cryptocurrency that will reward individuals for their BOIN contributions, and it can do this without needing a central authority to control or distribute these rewards.

Gridcoin is a bit different compared to some of the other cryptocurrencies on the market. It works on the same idea as other currencies, except that it allows users to help out the scientific community. With many users interested in helping out others and bettering our world, it is likely that this trend will continue to grow, making this a good currency to invest in.

Digibyte

Digibyte was released in 2014, but there wasn't a lot of fanfare that came along with it. This currency started out with low value, but this changed with the creation of Digisheild. This is an advanced alternative to the Kimoto Gravity Well, and it is now used by several other cryptocurrencies such as Dogecoin. This system is nice because it can protect the currencies from a large inflation from mining pools.

If you look through the communities for many altcoins, Digibyte has been credited for its adept team of developers who are working to help grow the network. They are mostly silent on social community and spend their time figuring out what the community wants. It currently has 14 or more mining pools, and it is already listed on nigh different digital currency exchanges, making it a top contender, even if the market cap is not as high as Bitcoin.

This is a good currency to go with. It has been around for a few years and is known to have a dedicated team to maintain it. It has a lower market cap than Bitcoin, but this makes it easier to enter the market because you will not need to come up with as much money to start. In addition, there are already many exchange sites and mining pools working with this currency, which shows that there is definitely some interest in this currency already.

The Burst Coin

BURST is the first to issue a coin that makes it easy to create smart contracts right out of your wallet. Smart contracts are a really neat part of the blockchain technology. These contracts are self-executing, which eliminates the need for a third-party to come in the middle of an agreement and charge a lot of money. They can be used for any kind of agreement, and once certain conditions are met, it will execute the agreements.

This coin also works with proof of capacity, which helps to keep it secure and easier to use compared to some of the others. BURST is known to use fewer resources than other currencies. This is because it will only read from your hard drive once for each block rather than multiple times. And it is not going to require a lot of big graphics cards that use a lot of energy to mine the coins.

This is a good currency to go with if you are interested in investing in smart contracts. Many individuals are tired of hiring a lawyer or other professional to complete a contract and then having to shell out thousands of dollars to get the contract complete.

With the help of smart contracts, such as the ones available with BURST, you can cut out the middleman and save the money. It is likely that many people will find this appealing in the future and the currencies that facilitate these smart contracts will definitely see an increase in their value.

Emercoin

Emercoin is a digital currency that relies on the blockchain technology. This blockchain provides services for personal and business use, no matter what you need to take care of. It has a secure shell management system that is needed by all the admins of the site as well as a system for authentication that does not require a password.

It also provides many other services that will help your business grow, al with the help of the great blockchain technology. Some of the other benefits and services that you can enjoy include:

Storage for your electronic business cards.
Trusted storage for all of your digital timestamps through the blockchain
A torrent tracker for all the file sharing that happens online
A decentralized pay per click advertising network.
A digital proof of ownership solution for digital and physical goods and services

This is a great currency to join if you are looking for an investment in blockchain technology. This one has been developed in a way to provide solutions for many types of businesses, allowing them to keep ownership over their products and services and making it easy to store their information and share files with everyone in their company. It has a broad application and is sure to grow in value as more businesses start to use it.

Peercoin

Peercoin, which also goes by the name of PPC or PPCoin, is known as a peer-to-peer cryptocurrency. It was developed in August 2012 by Sunny King and Scott Nadal. Sunny King is a pseudonym but is also known as one of the groups or individuals who helped to create Primecoin.

This currency may not be as old as Bitcoin, but it is still one of the earlier arrivals to the market. The average inflation rate for this currency has stayed below five percent as of 2014, and it is likely to stay close to that in the future. This is good news for the investor who is looking for a nice stable currency to work with.

It relies on the proof of stake and the proof of work protocols. The proof of stake means that it is not going to take a lot of computing power to keep the network secure. With proof of work, it helps to spread out the coins and how the coins are distributed. In addition, any of the hardware that has worked with Bitcoin will be able to help mine Peercoins, making it a good option to go with.

Nxt

You can also choose to work with the Nxt currency. This is a currency that is similar to Bitcoin in the fact that the blockchain technology is what helps to run this currency and keep it safe. This one is coded in Java so it is easy to work with and many programmers can check the code and make sure that it runs properly.

One benefit of using Nxt is that it is the first of the cryptocurrencies to rely only on proof of stake for consensus. This is a slightly different protocol for checking transactions, but it speeds up the process and can make it easier to use.

Many people will notice that the security of the wallet is a bit different than you will find with Bitcoin. Most clients will work with what is known as a bran wallet. With this, you will no longer need to store your keys in a wallet file. Instead, the security will work by a passphrase that the user needs to keep secret, making it easier to store your coins.

For those who are looking for an easier security currency, but still like the idea of working with the blockchain technology, Nxt may be the best option to invest in. It has a lot of the benefits of blockchain, some more neat features and is newer, allowing for more growth potential.

There are a few of the options that you can go with when you are ready to start investing in cryptocurrency. While some people focus on using Bitcoin or Ethereum, others will look for valuable new currencies because these have more potential to grow. If you are looking for a newer coin to invest in, then take a look through this list to help you get started.

Chapter 10: Why Now is the Time to Invest in Cryptocurrencies

So, the next question that you may be asking yourself is why now? Why is now the perfect time to join in on all this cryptocurrency craze? Would it be better to wait it out and see what happens to these currencies before you decide to join the market? How long are these markets going to be good for anyway? Are you going to put all of your money into the market and find out these currencies fail within a few months?

The truth is, there is no better time to join the cryptocurrency market than right now. While it may seem like these currencies are all over the news right now, there are still a lot of people who have never heard of any of them. However, the major consensus on these coins is that they are exactly what the consumer needs.

Each day, more and more people join these networks and start to use these cryptocurrencies. Sometimes they go for one of the big names, especially if they want to send and receive money rather than investing, but sometimes they also go for some of the smaller options depending on their needs.

This market is sure to grow. There are so many people all around the world who have yet to hear and try out these cryptocurrencies. This means that as these people start to join the market, the value of cryptocurrency will continue to go up.

If you have already invested in the cryptocurrency, especially if you are going with a long-term investment strategy, then this is good news for you. The more the value of those currencies increases, the more profit it will make. Getting into cryptocurrencies now can put you in a prime location for earning more in the future.

At some point though, these currencies will start leveling out. They are new right now and still have a lot of markets open to them so the value will keep going up. But at some point, they will stop going up and will reach an equilibrium like with other fiat currencies.

This will happen sometime in the future. It could be in the next few years, or it could be longer down the road. All guesses and claims are just predictions right now, and no one knows when these currencies will start to lose value or at least equal out.

Waiting too long to get into the cryptocurrency market could end up losing you money. If the market evens out or goes down, shortly after you make your investment, then you will not make any money in the process. You need to get in when the market is really good if you want to make any money in cryptocurrencies.

While some people think that these cryptocurrencies are all in a bubble and will soon be gone, there are a lot of neat features about them that can help at least a few of them to stay around into the future. Right now is the best time to get into cryptocurrency investing.

There is a lot of interest in the market, lots of room for the market to grow, and the value keeps going up and up. If you have ever considered starting out with this type of investment, then it is time to get moving and start investing today.

Conclusion

Thank you for making it through to the end of this book, let's hope it was informative and able to provide you with all of the tools you need to achieve your goals whatever they may be.

The next step is to decide if investing in cryptocurrency is the right choice for you to go with. There are many investment types, but right now, working in cryptocurrencies is one of the most profitable, and low-risk, investment options that you can go with. The goal of this guidebook was to provide you with all of the information that you need to successfully invest in cryptocurrencies.

Inside this guidebook, you were able to learn some of the basics about cryptocurrencies and how to get started in this market. Then we moved on to talking about some of the most common cryptocurrencies and how they play into the market to help with your investment. And finally, you will also learn some of the best strategies that come with investing in most cryptocurrencies, whether you are a beginner investor or someone who has been investing for a long time.

The more information that you have about cryptocurrency, the easier it is to make smart investing decisions. Make sure to check out this guidebook to help you learn about cryptocurrency and to get started on the right track to see success.

Finally, if you found this book useful in anyway, a review on Amazon is always appreciated!

Description

This innovative investor's guide to an entirely new asset class will open your mind to the endless possibilities of crypto currency and bitcoin investing. There is a great wealth that will be made over the next 5 years for those brave enough to understand and invest in this new and emerging technology!

Once only used to buy items on the black market bitcoin investing and blockhain technology is now a investors dream! Now is the greatest time in history to capitalize on bitcoin investing with virtual currency being the greatest investment opportunity since the Internet invention itself.

Bitcoin pathed the way for crypto currency introducing the world to the idea of virtual money and all its possibilities. Now today there are over 800 and counting crypto currency, including ether, ripple, litecoin, monero, and more.

Bitcoin investing will give you a clear and concise guide **providing you with an in-depth look at cryptocurrencies and how to get started investing in them. We will take a look at all aspects of cryptocurrencies, including what they are, who some of the big players in the market are, and how to invest in the market.**

There is so much to learn and understand about this market, and we will cover it in this bitcoin guidebook.

This guide will gives you all the tools you need:

- What is cryptocurrency
- What is the blockchain technology
- What you need to know about the big names in the game including Bitcoin, Litecoin, Ripple, and Ethereum
- How to actually do bitcoin investing
- How to pick and value a coin to invest in
- The history of crypto currency. Must know to avoid the next bubble
- How to make money day trading crypto currency
- How the buy and hold strategy can make you a lot of money
- Why now is the best time invest in these currencies

As well as all this the author will give you reliable smart investment strategies for bitcoing investing as well as other up and coming currency and smart block chain technology. By understanding the technology, it history, present and future you can be clear on your investment strategies making sure you your investments are of sound decisions.

If you're ready to catch the Crypto currency wave and make a fortune in the process, then this is book to read. Pick it up today before you miss the wave and get left behind!

www.ingramcontent.com/pod-product-compliance
Lightning Source LLC
Chambersburg PA
CBHW071207220526
45468CB00002B/536